spanish for homebuyers

teach yourself®

spanish for homebuyers

peter and nat macbride

with eva mendaro carrió

for over 60 years, more than 50 million people have learnt over 750 subjects the **teach yourself** way, with impressive results.

be where you want to be with **teach yourself**

The publisher has used its best endeavours to ensure that the URLs referred to in this book are correct and active at the time of going to press. However, the publisher and the author have no responsibilities for the websites and can make no guarantee that a site will remain live or that the content will remain relevant, decent or appropriate.

For UK order enquiries: please contact Bookpoint Ltd, 130 Milton Park, Abingdon, Oxon OX14 4SB. Telephone: +44 (0)1235 827720. Fax: +44 (0)1235 400454. Lines are open 09.00–17.00, Monday to Saturday, with a 24-hour message answering service. Details about our titles and how to order are available at www.teachyourself.co.uk.

Long renowned as the authoritative source for self-guided learning – with more than 50 million copies sold worldwide – the **teach yourself** series includes over 500 titles in the fields of languages, crafts, hobbies, business, computing and education.

British Library Cataloguing in Publication Data.
A catalogue record for this title is available from The British Library.

Library of Congress Catalog Number: on file.

First published in UK 2005 by Hodder Education, 338 Euston Road, London, NW1 3BH.
This edition published 2007.

Typeset by MacDesign, Southampton

Printed in Great Britain for Hodder Education, an Hachette Livre UK Company, 338 Euston Road, London NW1 3BH by Cox & Wyman Ltd, Reading, Berkshire.

Hodder Headline's policy is to use papers that are natural, renewable and recyclable products and made from wood grown in sustainable forests. The logging and manufacturing processes are expected to conform to the environmental regulations of the country of origin.

Impression number 10 9 8 7 6 5 4 3 2 1

Year 2011 2010 2009 2008 2007

contents

preface

The thought behind this book is a simple one. If you want to buy a house in Spain, it helps if you know the words. This isn't the same as being able to speak Spanish – even with a degree in Spanish, you may not know your *contrato de compraventa* (contract of sale) from your *alero* (eaves). No, you don't actually have to be able to speak Spanish – though it helps no end if you do – but if you know the words that describe houses and their various components, and the words that are involved in the sale process, then you will be better equipped for finding, buying and settling into your Spanish home.

Teach Yourself Spanish for homebuyers covers over 1,200 of the most useful words for home buyers and home owners, but this book is not a dictionary. A translation alone is sometimes not enough. It doesn't get you much further to know that *notario* translates to 'notary', or that *falleba* means 'shutter fastener'. You need to know what the *notario*'s role is and how it affects you, and what a *falleba* looks like. The words are given here in the context of the buying process or of different aspects of the house. Where it will help, we've tried to explain the concepts behind the words or to give an illustration.

We couldn't have produced this book without the assistance of our Spanish experts, Eva Mendaro Carrió and Charles Balfour, and our illustrator Tony Jones of Art Construction. Thanks are also due to Alexandra Jaton and Ginny Catmur of Hodder and Stoughton, and to Catherine McGregor, our copy-editor; and to our friends and neighbours in France and Spain.

Peter and Nat MacBride
Southampton, Miramont de Guyenne and Barcelona, 2007

The CD

The CD that accompanies this book is designed to be used alongside Chapter 10, *una hora de español – an hour of Spanish*. There are 20 tracks:

Track 1 is a very brief introduction to the Spanish language, covering pronunciation, how to greet people, ask questions and understand simple replies.

The remaining tracks all give practice in speaking and listening to some of the most important or useful words in each chapter. It should take between 5 and 15 minutes to complete each one – work through a track before going out to tackle a job and you will be better prepared to deal with the *agencias* and the *artesanos*.

Track 2 links to Chapter 1, *La búsqueda – the search*

Track 3 links to Chapter 2, *La venta – the sale*

Track 4 links to Chapter 3, *Las obras – building work*

Tracks 5–7 link to Chapter 4, *La estructura – the structure*

Track 5: *Talking to el albañil – the builder*

Track 6: *Finding tools and materials at the bricolaje*

Track 7: *Talking to el carpintero – the carpenter and el tejador – the roofer*

Tracks 8–10 link to Chapter 5, *La carpintería – woodwork*

Track 8: *Talking to el carpintero – the joiner*

Track 9: *Finding materials at the bricolaje*

Track 10: *Finding tools at the bricolaje*

Tracks 11–13 link to Chapter 6, *La fontanería – plumbing*

Track 11: *Talking to el fontanero – the plumber*

Track 12: *Shopping for bathroom and kitchen equipment*

Track 13: *Finding tools at the bricolaje*

Tracks 14–15 link to Chapter 7, *La calefacción y la electricidad – heating and electricity*

Track 14: *Talking to el ingeniero de calefacción – the heating engineer*

Track 15: *Shopping for los electrodomésticos – electrical appliances*

Tracks 16–18 link to Chapter 8, *La decoración – decorating*

Track 16: *Finding materials at the bricolaje*

Track 17: *Finding tools at the bricolaje*

Track 18: *Finding floor coverings, curtains and furniture*

Tracks 19–20 link to Chapter 9, *El jardín – the garden*

Track 19: *Talking to los albañiles – the builders*

Track 20: *Shopping for el jardín – the garden*

The voices on the CD are those of Marisa Julián and Stuart Nurse.

01 la búsqueda – the search

Almost the same...

In Spain as in the UK, property is usually sold through *agencias inmobiliarias* (estate agents), though private sales are more common than here. You often see *se vende* (for sale) signs attached to gate posts or lamp posts around the area, or even *se vende* slips tucked under the windscreen wipers of cars. This is probably a reflection of the very high rates of commission charged by Spanish estate agents – anything from 5 to 25%!

Until 2000, agents had to be registered with a professional body, either GIPE (*Gestores Intermediarios en Promociones de Edficaciones* – Building Promotion Intermediaries) or API (*Agentes de la Propiedad Inmobiliaria* – Property Agents). This is no longer the case, and as might be expected in a market with such mouthwatering profits, there are cowboys. If you're using agents, look for GIPE or API accreditation (see page 8).

Once you get there, Spanish agents are much the same as those in the UK. The main difference is that you won't be set upon by an eager salesperson the moment you set foot inside! There is often a secretary, and you may have to sit down and wait for an agent to get off the phone (they *can* talk, the Spanish, oh yes!). You will find that most agents are professional and friendly, know their properties well and can talk intelligently about them. As well as printed information sheets, they may well have extra photos and information on computer which they'll be happy to show you. If you find any of interest, they will print copies of the sheets, and arrange a visit if you want one.

But before we get into an agent's office, we have to find one! Let's start the search.

Define your search

Where do you want to buy? In which region? In a big town, a village, an *urbanización* (purpose-built development) or rural isolation? Beach or mountains? What sort and size of property do you want? A flat, a small cottage or a plush villa? Do you want a garden or a terrace? What about a pool – private or communal? How much work do you want to have to do on it? Are you looking for a ruin to rebuild, an old house to restore, one that needs a little light redecorating, or a new build?

These are questions that only you can answer – this checklist may help you to define your ideal house.

Ideal house checklist

Location: Province or region ....

Beach, mountains or other? ....

City, village, *urbanización* or countryside? ....

Is the view important? ....

Max distance from shops ....

Max distance from cafés/restaurants ....

Max distance from beach/swimming/etc. ....

Max distance from children's play facilities ....

Size: Number of bedrooms ....

Other rooms ....

Minimum total floorspace ....

Outside: Swimming pool? (None/Communal/Private) ......

Garage/parking needed? (Y/N) ....

Garden/land? (None/Communal/Private) ....

Minimum garden/land area ....

Condition: New build, or resale? (1) ....

Ruin/renovation/redecoration/ready? (2) ....

What furniture/fittings are present? ....

Budget: How much money is available? ....

How much time do you have? (3) ....

(1) Fees and taxes will add approx. 5% to the cost of a new house and 10% to the cost of a resale (see pages 37–8).

(2) If you plan to rebuild or restore, you must have some idea of the cost of building work and be prepared to deal with the paperwork (see Chapter 3).

(3) The less time you have to work on the house, the more professional services you will have to buy.

The regions of Spain

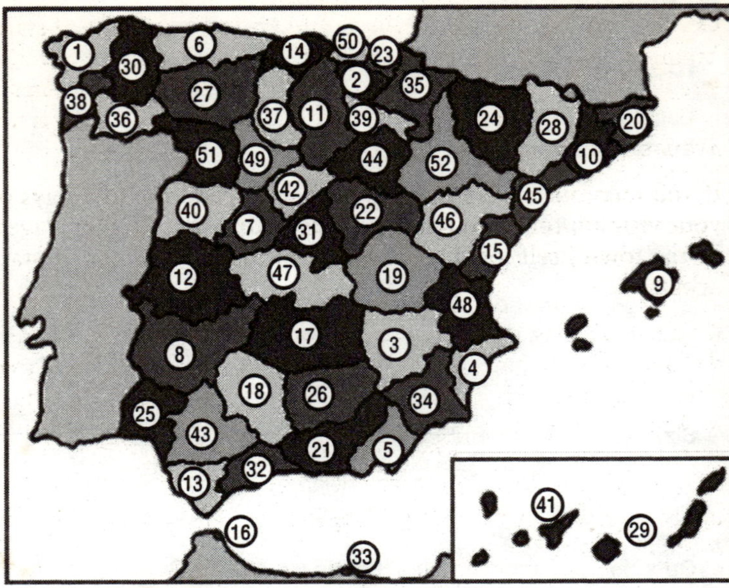

1 Aco – La Coruña
2 Ala – Álava
3 Alb – Albacete
4 Ali – Alicante
5 Alm – Almería
6 Ast – Asturias
7 Avi – Ávila
8 Bad – Badajoz
9 Bal – Islas Baleares
10 Bar – Barcelona
11 Bur – Burgos
12 Cac – Cáceres
13 Cad – Cádiz
14 Can – Cantabria
15 Cas – Castellón
16 Ceu – Ceuta
17 Ciu – Ciudad Real
18 Cor – Córdoba
19 Cue – Cuenca
20 Gir – Girona
21 Gra – Granada
22 Gua – Guadalajara
23 Gui – Guipúzcoa
24 Hca – Huesca
25 Hva – Huelva
26 Jae – Jaén
27 Leo – León
28 Lle – Lleida
29 Lpa – Las Palmas de Gran Canaria
30 Lug – Lugo
31 Mad – Madrid
32 Mal – Málaga
33 Mel – Melilla
34 Mur – Murcia
35 Nav – Navarra
36 Our – Ourense
37 Pal – Palencia
38 Pon – Pontevedra
39 Rio – La Rioja
40 Sal – Salamanca
41 Sct – Santa Cruz De Tenerife
42 Seg – Segovia
43 Sev – Sevilla
44 Sor – Soria
45 Tar – Tarragona
46 Ter – Teruel
47 Tol – Toledo
48 Vlc – Valencia
49 Vld – Valladolid
50 Viz – Vizcaya
51 Zam – Zamorra
52 Zar – Zaragoza

Searching through the web

Get online before you leave home and give yourself a head start. You may be able to find your house through the web, but even if you don't find a specific one, you will find the more active agents and get a good idea of the prices and the kind of properties available in an area.

If you miss out the web search, you will spend the first days of your visit hunting through the *Páginas Amarillas* (Yellow Pages) or the town itself looking for the *agencias inmobiliarias* (estate agents).

If you're looking for a new-build home in an *urbanización* (residential development), you are probably best going to a UK-based site, since these are built mainly for foreign owners. If you're looking for a resale property in a town or in the countryside, find a Spanish agent. Some UK-based agents do offer resale properties, but will probably have a limited range, and you are less likely to pick up a bargain – these sites are aimed at well-heeled foreigners, after all.

UK-based property sites

As well as advertising houses, these offer varying levels of help with buying and settling in, e.g. arranging mortgages, translating legal documents, linking with English-speaking craftsmen. The main limitation, of course, is that they only have a tiny proportion of the houses on the market – most UK-based agents specialise in a particular area or work exclusively with one developer.

If you have a very clear idea of where you want to be, try typing 'property spain' and the name of the place into a search engine and you will almost certainly find a number of UK-based agents operating in that area. If the type of property and location is more important than a specific place, try looking on an 'umbrella' site – one which deals with properties from many different agents.

There is no shortage of sites dealing with Spanish property, so set aside some time to explore the web, but to get you started, here are some that you may find useful:

- **The Move Channel** advertises properties for agents across Spain, giving brief details and passing on requests for further information to the agents. You need to register with them to make requests. Find them at: **http://spain.themovechannel.com**

- **Spanish Inland Properties** are specialists in – as you might expect from the name – village houses and fincas in the countryside. Find them at: **www.spanish-inland-properties.com**

- **Kyero** has details of thousands of properties, including plenty of old country *cortijos* and *fincas* in need of restoration. Most properties are near the coasts, or in inland areas in the south. Details are sometimes brief, but the location maps, climate and price index information are all handy. Find them at: **www.kyero.com**

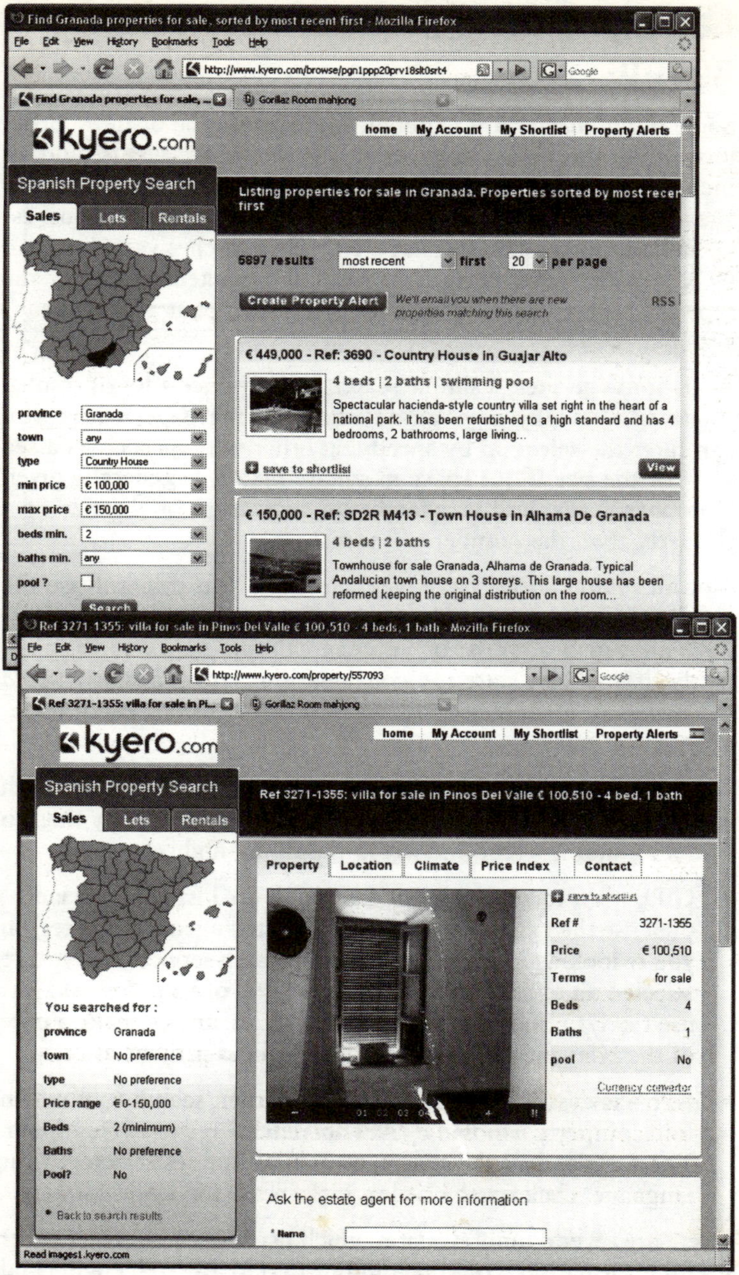

Kyero has a wide range of properties throughout Spain.

Las agencias inmobiliarias – estate agents

Some *inmobiliarias* are national, some cover one or more provinces and others are purely local. All the larger agents, and an increasing number of the small ones, have web sites, and most sites have a search facility. Many will have English versions, especially in the popular coastal areas. The searches vary, but tend to follow the same pattern – you will be asked to specify the type of property, price range and region (except at a local agent's site).

At nationwide sites, a simple search can produce a lot of results. These sites usually have an advanced search page, where you can filter the selection by specifying other options such as a sea view or the size (floor space in square metres is generally given in property ads, and is a far better indication of the size of a property than the number of rooms).

Not all *inmobiliarias* have web sites, but you can still use the web to find the ones in your area. They will probably at least have an e-mail address, or you can call and speak to them directly. If you can start the conversation with *Disculpe, habla usted inglés?* (excuse me, do you speak English?), you'll probably get on fine!

To find a Spanish *inmobiliaria*, you are best starting your search with one of the professional bodies – you're more likely then to find a reputable agent and avoid the fly-by-nights.

- GIPE – go to **www.gipe.es** and click on **Listado Asociados**, then use the map to find GIPE accredited agents in the region you're looking in. GIPE also offers a search service once you've selected an agent, but it isn't a great deal of help. I would just use GIPE to find agents in the area you're after – make a note of the relevant companies and then contact them directly.
- API – **www.comprarcasa.com** has its own search tool which finds property handled by API-accredited agents across Spain. The site also has an English version – if it doesn't detect your language, click on the Union Jack in the top right corner.

There are several umbrella sites which list agencies or offer other useful information – or you could just go to a search engine and type in 'inmobiliaria' and the area you're interested in.

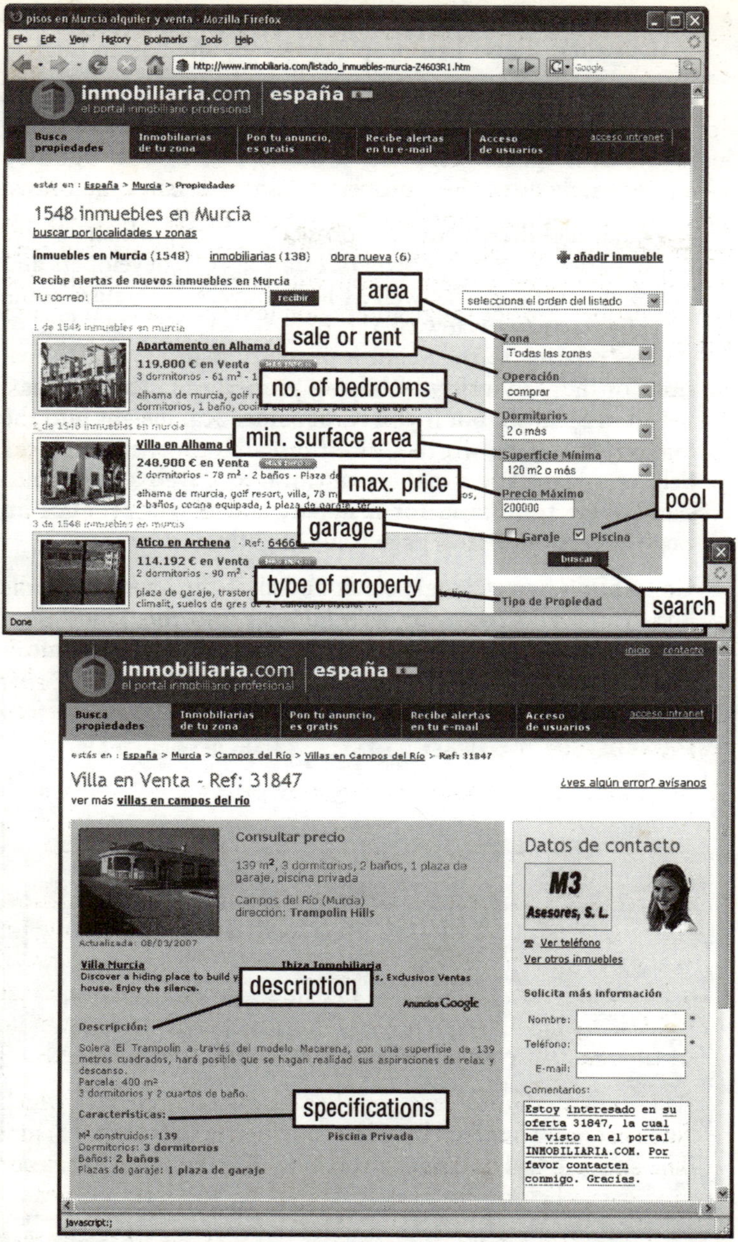

Searching at inmobiliaria.com – the better sites all work in much the same way. With a little vocabulary you can run a search and make sense of the results.

- **www.inmobiliaria.com** lists agents by region, and has links to their sites. It also lists properties itself, and has an English version of the property details (well, half-English – there's an English summary, followed by specifications in Spanglish).
- **www.inmonegocios.com** lists a number of agents, but also has privately advertised properties. Spanish language only.
- **www.lainmobiliaria.org** is a property portal, which invites participation from homeowners, estate agents, developers and building contractors as well as homebuyers. There are some classified ads (very few at the time of writing), but lots of articles relating to the Spanish property market, and discussions of the nitty-gritty of buying properties in the forums. It's all in Spanish, but if you want some local insight into the market, it may be worth a bit of research time, enlisting the help of a translation tool – you can feed a web address into the Google translator, for instance, and it will produce an English version of any page (only slightly garbled!).

  Go to **http://www.google.co.uk** and click the **Language tools** link. Copy and paste the web address into the **Translate a web page** box, select **Spanish to English** and hit **Translate.**

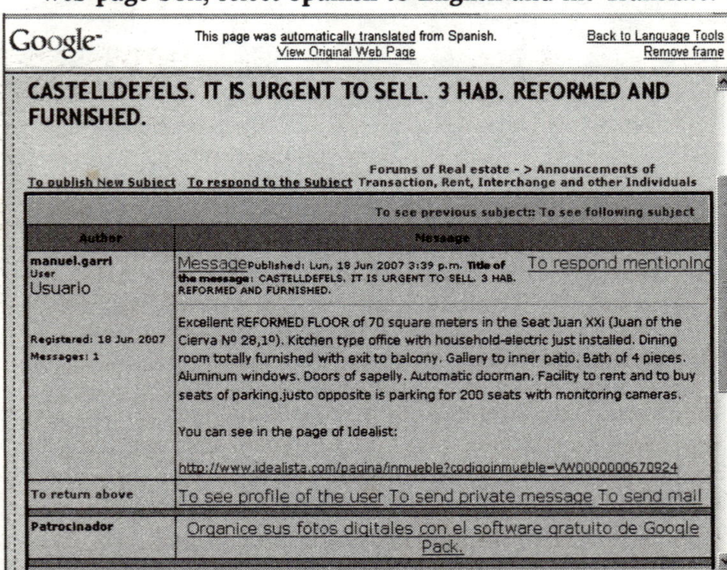

The outcome from a Google translation. You may have to work a little to follow some of the text, but it is a good way to get local knowledge.

Agents as searchers

Some agents offer e-mail update services, that will compare your search against new properties and alert you of any that may be suitable. Others will invite you to e-mail your requirements and will search beyond the properties visible on-line. Given the huge commissions paid to agents, I'd take advantage of these services where you can – make them earn their money! – especially if you are short of time for searching on the ground.

Search on the ground

When you plan your buying trip, allow at least twice as much time as you think is really necessary. Delays can happen, and if everything does go smoothly, you can relax and treat the rest of your stay as a simple holiday.

If you have found potential houses on the web, contact the *inmobiliarias* by e-mail or phone to arrange to visit them. Allow plenty of time for each visit. The agencies may have other properties – newly-in or not advertised online – that you may want to see, and each house viewing can take a while.

Use the *Páginas Amarillas* (Yellow Pages) directory to find the other local agents and notarios and see what they have to offer. And keep an eye out for *se vende* (for sale) signs outside houses.

Trees can also get pressed into service as 'For sale' billboards.

New houses

Renovating an ancient old farmhouse is not everybody's idea of fun. New houses have nice fitted kitchens and sparkling bathrooms; they will be freshly painted and decorated throughout to your specifications; and if you have been involved from an early enough stage, the layout and the number, size and types of rooms may have been customised to your liking. And, of course, if you start from scratch with a plot of land and your own builder, then the house will be exactly as you want it (if all goes to plan...).

EN VENTA

ATIS REAL Auguste-Thouard España Residencial

EIXAMPLE

Location: Eixample is a smart area of Barcelona

- **Sobreático de 112 m²**
  (Terraza incluída)
- **2 Habitaciones** — 2 bedrooms
- **1 Baño** — 1 bathroom
- **Cocina Office** — kitchen/breakfast room

4.90.000 €

- **Ascensor** — lift
- **Exterior** — outward-facing – no rooms without exterior windows
- **Mucho sol y luz** — very light and sunny
- **Impecable** — perfect condition

C. BAILEN / C. ARAGON

TEL. 93.342.49.63 / FAX. 93.301.08.01

Typical information sheet from a Spanish estate agent – the price had been changed, which is why it was hand-written. This is a shifting market, but prices can go down as well as up!

If you don't know where you want to be, or what sort of house, spend more time exploring Spain, renting different types of houses in different areas, then start looking.

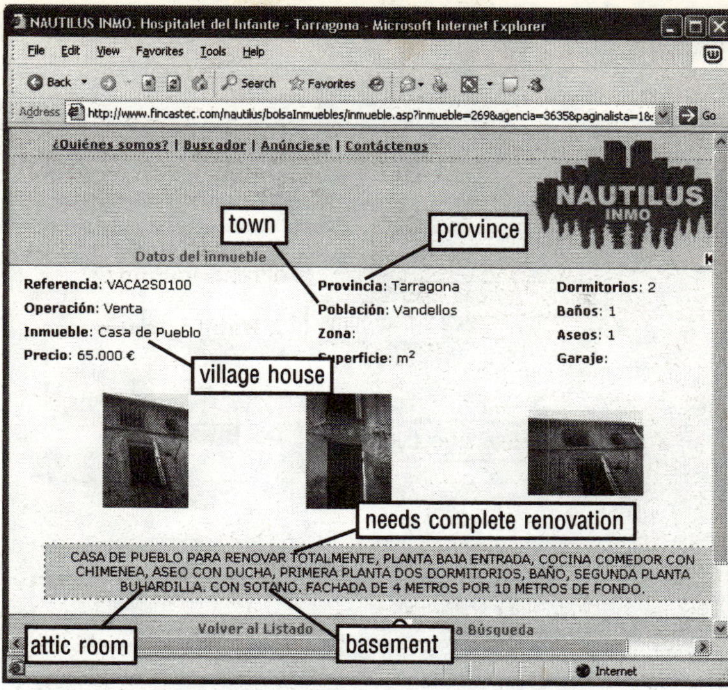

Here's a full restoration project for someone keen – two storeys plus an attic room and basement, and an open fire in the kitchen/diner.

New houses should have guarantees on electrical and structural work, and there are some financial advantages to buying a new home. There is no property transfer tax to pay (normally 6%), just stamp duty at 0.5%. New houses are subject to VAT, but this is currently only 7%, compared to 16% for all other building work. When you are quoted a price for a new house, ask if it includes IVA – *Impuesto sobre el Valor Añadido* (VAT).

Inspection tours

The property sites and *inmobiliarias* deal with new houses as well as old ones, but there are of course all those agents who specialise in new builds. This kind of agent will frequently offer the infamous inspection tour – a subsidised trip to Spain to see show homes, where you will face varying degrees of pressure to sign on the dotted line before you go home.

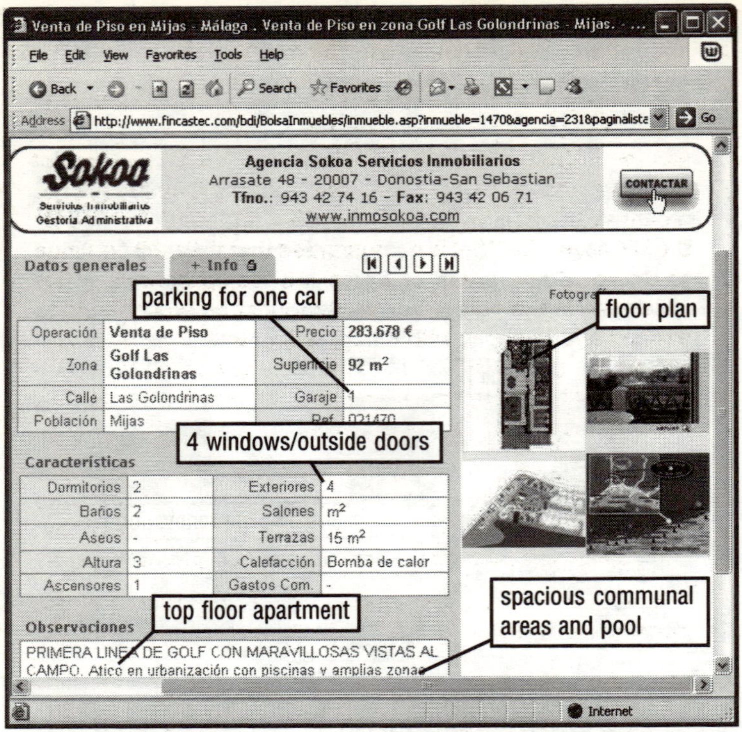

And at the other end of the scale, here's a new-build apartment on the edge of a golf course – hurry, it's the last one in this phase of construction!

Reputable firms really won't push too hard – they know that the trips pay off their investment anyway, and the less they bully you, the more likely you are to recommend them to your friends. They'll slap 'Hurry! Only a few villas left!' notices all over their brochures, but won't actually twist your arm too hard when you're over in Spain looking at them.

Others will bombard you with commission-hungry reps who will do absolutely everything they can to get you committed, and we sincerely hope you do not find yourself on such a tour. If you do, just hold firm and don't do anything until you've got home and had a chance to think calmly about it all. That perfect villa which is apparently about to be sold under your nose to someone else will almost certainly still be there when you get back.

Buying as an investment?

Some people do buy houses in Spain more as investments than for their own use, hoping for capital growth or rental income or both. If this is your plan, you should be aware of the following: house prices have gone up significantly in recent years, as they have in the UK – and partly fuelled by the UK rises – but that is no guarantee that they will continue to do so. Some areas of Spain are facing serious water shortages in the near future as its tourist areas continue to expand and multiply, with thirsty golf courses, gardens and swimming pools to supply. This may threaten the rental market – or strengthen it, if restrictions are placed on new building instead of on water usage.

Then there are of course the difficulties of managing a property from afar – what happens when things break and need fixing? How far do you trust the letting agents? Can you cover the costs during periods without guests/tenants?

There's more on buying property as in investment in the appendix (page 179).

Lexicon: la búsqueda – the search

agencia inmobiliaria (f)*	estate agent
anterior	previous
buscar	to search (e.g. at a web site)
búsqueda (f)	search
casa (f)	house
compra (f)	purchase
comprar	to buy
habitación (f)	room
joven	recently built
moderno	modern
nueva	new
nueva búsqueda (f)	new search

* All nouns are either masculine (m) or feminine (f) – see page 155. Some are always plural, shown by (mpl) or (fpl). e.g. you can't have 'a plier'.

para renovar	needs renovating
se vende	for sale
siguiente	next
terreno (m)	land
venta (f)	sale

Inmobiliaria abbreviations

A/A	aire acondicionado	air conditioning
apto	apartamento	apartment
asc	ascensor	lift
calef	calefacción	central heating
carp alu	carpintería de aluminio	aluminium window frames
coc	cocina	kitchen
com	comedor	dining room
fca	finca	building
hab	habitaciones	rooms
or	orientación	which way the property faces
p.b.	planta baja	ground floor
PEV	para entrar a vivir	ready to be lived in
pl	planta	storey – e.g. *5ª pl = 5th storey*
ref	reformado	refurbished
sal	sala de estar	lounge
urb	urbanización	housing development

How many rooms?

Be careful about how you interpret the word *habitaciones* in property adverts. Usually it refers to the number of bedrooms, but *habitación* actually just means 'room', so double-check with the agent.

Lexicon: los tipos de viviendas – types of houses

a estrenar	ready for habitation
apartamento (m)	flat
ático (m)	top-floor apartment – usually has a larger terrace
buen estado (m)	good condition
casa (f)	house
casa adosada	terraced house/semi
casa de pueblo	village house
casa independiente	detached house
cerca del mar	near the sea
chalet (m)	detached house/villa
con/sin luz	with/without electricity
cortijo (m)	country property, laid out around a central courtyard
domicilio (m)	residence
edificio (m)	building
finca (f)	building – with a flat, the kind of building it's in may be mentioned.
finca regial	very luxurious apartment building – expect marble floors, plenty of wrought ironwork and probably a concierge
finca rústica	country house
finca señorial	luxury apartment building
granja (f)	farm
ideal inversores	ideal investment property
masía (f)	large country residence or mansion
molino (m)	mill
necesita mejoras	needs some improvements
orientado al mar/montañas	facing the sea/mountains
para entrar a vivir	ready to be lived in

para reformar	for refurbishment
para renovar	for renovation (this can mean complete rebuild!)
piso (m)	flat
reformado	refurbished
ruina (f)	ruin – expect to knock it down and start from scratch
rústico	in the country
solar (m)	building plot
terreno rústico (m)	agricultural land – usually with permission to build a farmhouse
terreno urbanizable (m)	building land
¡véalo!	has to be seen!
viejo	old
villa (m)	modern house (usually detached)
vistas (fpl)	(good) views
vivienda (f)	house/home

Lexicon: las habitaciones y características – rooms and features

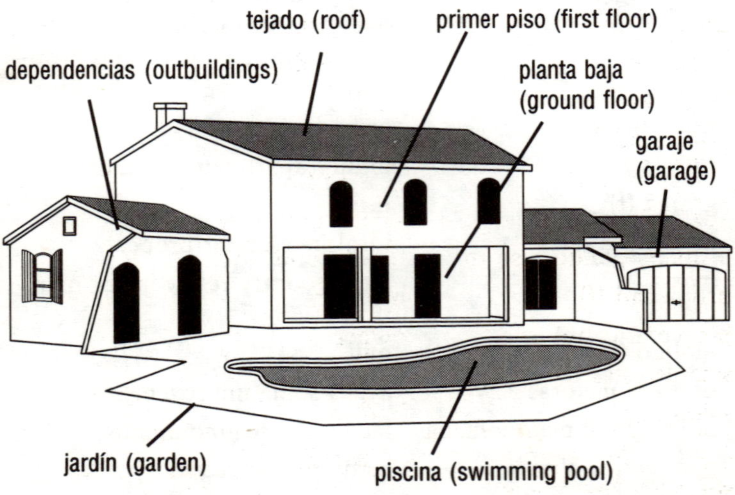

almacén (m)	storeroom
alimentación (f)	supply (water, electricity, etc.)
aseo (m)	lavatory
balcón (m)	balcony
bodega (f)	cellar
chimenea (f)	chimney/fireplace
cocina (f)	kitchen
cocina americana	open-plan kitchen
cocina office	kitchen/breakfast room
comedor (m)	dining room
comunitario	communal
cuarto de baño (m)	bathroom
de diseño	designer
dependencia (f)	outbuilding
despacho (m)	study
despensa (f)	storeroom
desván (m)	attic/loft
dormitorio (m)	bedroom
fosa séptica (f)	septic tank
garaje (m)	garage
gastos (mpl) de comunidad	service charges
granero (m)	storeroom
habitación (f)	room/bedroom
jardín (m)	garden
piscina (f)	swimming pool
planta baja (f)	ground floor
pozo séptico (m)	septic tank
primer/segundo piso (m)	first/second floor
propiedad (f)	property
propietario (m)	owner
sala de estar (f)	living room
salón (m)	lounge
sótano (m)	basement
suelo gres/parqué (m)	stone/parquet floor

tejado (m)	roof
terraza (f)	terrace
terreno (m)	grounds
todo exterior	'all outside' – many flats have rooms with no external windows; this means every room has one
trastero (m)	utility room

What's included in the price?

If the house is furnished when you view it, ask very carefully about what will be included in the sale price. It is not unusual for the vendor to remove everything that isn't screwed down and quite a lot of what is. The bath, toilet and other sanitaryware are usually left, but the kitchen fittings – including the sink – may be taken, along with garden ornaments, shelves, carpets, curtains, light bulbs...

If there is anything in the house that you would like to be there when it becomes yours, tell the agent or the vendor, agree a price and get it written into the initial contract. Most vendors are open to reasonable offers. They're not trying to rip you off – it's just a different way of doing things.

Found it?

You've found a place that's perfect, or as near as perfect as you can get within your budget. What next? There are three key questions that need answering:

- Is it worth the asking price?
- Is it really within your budget?
- If you intend to adapt, improve or extend the house, will you be allowed to do it?

To get the answers, ask the experts.

El perito – the valuer

Your *abogado* (lawyer) or a *perito tasador* (valuation expert) will also check a number of other factors which may affect the cost of the property. These include:

- The land owned with the property. Old houses, especially in villages, often have one or more non-adjacent gardens or other plots of land. The expert will check the *Catastro* – the official map that shows the boundaries and ownership of land in the area.
- The planning status of the area, as shown in the local PGOU (*Plan General de Ordenación Urbana*) – planning brief. This will tell you what future development may happen in the area around the house, and whether you will be able to adapt the house in the way you want to. We will have another look at the PGOU in Chapter 3.
- Any rights of way or other encumbrances on the property.

Just as in the UK, you would be well advised to get a survey done on any property more than a few years old – we had a friend in Barcelona who was saddled with a €12,000 bill for shoring up the front of her flat when she discovered that that nice fresh plaster on the wall was just covering up the cracks...

The 'Spanish Land Grab' Law

You may have heard talk of the dreaded 'Spanish Land Grab' law which allows local authorities to expropriate part of your property with minimal compensation. There is some truth in the tale, though it's not as bad as people like to make out. New developments require infrastructure to supply them with water, electricity, sewerage, etc. Tourism is an important part of the Spanish economy, so laws were introduced to make sure that a landowner could not hold the local government to ransom over building essential improvements across their land. In most of the country, there has been no problem with the law – it is used infrequently, only where necessary, and with plenty of warning. Unfortunately, the law was badly drawn up in the province of Valencia, and some unscrupulous councils and developers took advantage of this. Wherever you are buying, but especially if you are buying in this area, make sure you get your *abogado* to check up on your vulnerability to expropriation.

Los presupuestos - estimates

If there are limited jobs to do, e.g. a new roof, new bathroom, rewiring, etc. you can ask local tradesmen for a *presupuesto* (estimate). You can rely on a *presupuesto* to give you an accurate cost of the finished work – as long as you take it up within a few months, and don't redefine the job. For more complicated work, approach an *arquitecto* (architect). As well as drawing up the plans, Spanish architects will get estimates and oversee the building job. We will come back to the *arquitecto* and *presupuesto* in Chapter 3 when we look at building work.

English–Spanish quick reference

The search - la búsqueda

buy	comprar
estate agent	agencia inmobiliaria (f)
for sale	se vende
house	casa (f)
land	terreno (m)
modern	moderno
needs renovating	para renovar
new search	nueva búsqueda (f)
next	siguiente
previous	anterior
purchase	compra (f)
recently built	joven, nuevo
room	habitación (f)
sale	venta (f)
search (noun)	búsqueda (f)
search (verb)	buscar

Types of houses – los tipos de vivienda

agricultural land	terreno rústico (m)
building	finca (f), edificio (m)

building land	terreno urbanizable (m)
building plot	solar (m)
country house	finca rústica (f)
courtyard-style house	cortijo (m)
detached house	casa independiente (f)/chalet (m)
facing the sea/mountains	orientado al mar/montañas
farm	granja (f)
flat	apartamento (m)/piso (m)
for refurbishment	para reformar
for renovation	para renovar
good condition	buen estado (m)
(good) views	vistas (fpl)
grand apartment building	finca regial (f)
house	casa (f)
house/home	vivienda (f)
housing development	urbanización
ideal investment property	ideal inversores
in the country	rústico, rural
large country residence	masía (f)
luxury apartment building	finca señorial (f)
mill	molino (m)
modern house	villa (m)
near the sea	cerca del mar
needs some improvements	necesita mejoras
old	viejo
ready to be lived in	a estrenar/para entrar a vivir
refurbished	reformado
residence	domicilio (m), residencia (f)
ruin	ruina (f)
terraced house/semi	casa adosada (f)
top-floor apartment	ático (m)
village house	casa (f) de pueblo
with/without electricity	con/sin luz

Rooms and facilities – las habitaciones y las características

air conditioning	aire acondicionado (m)
aluminium window frames	carpintería (f) de aluminio
apartment	apartamento (m)
attic/loft	desván (m)
balcony	balcón (m)
basement	sótano (m)
bathroom	cuarto de baño (m)
bedroom	dormitorio (m)
cellar	bodega (f)
central heating	calefacción
chimney/fireplace	chimenea (f)
communal	comunitario
dining room	comedor (m)
floor (first/second)	(primer/segundo) piso (m)
garage	garaje (m)
garden	jardín (m)
ground floor	planta baja (f)
grounds	terreno (m)
kitchen	cocina (f)
kitchen/breakfast room	cocina (f) office
lavatory	aseo (m)
lift	ascensor (m)
living room	sala (f) de estar
lounge	salón (m)/sala (f) de estar
open-plan kitchen	cocina americana (f)
outbuilding	dependencia (f)
owner	propietario (m)
property	propiedad (f)
refurbished	reformado
room/bedroom	habitación (f)
septic tank	fosa séptica (f), pozo séptico (m)

service charges	gastos (mpl) de comunidad
stone/parquet floor	suelo gres/parqué (m)
storeroom	despensa (f)
storey	planta/piso
study	despacho (m)
supply (water, etc.)	alimentación (f)
swimming pool	piscina (f)
terrace	terraza (f)
utility room	trastero (m)

02 la venta – the sale

Almost the same...

When you buy a house in England or Wales, nothing is certain until you exchange contracts, close to the end of the process. In Spain you and the seller are both heavily committed to the terms of the sale at the very beginning. You cannot be gazumped in Spain, neither buyer nor seller can renegotiate the price, nor can either of you back out without paying hefty compensation, unless there's a very good reason. A sale may only be cancelled if agreed conditions are not met or if a mortgage cannot be obtained. The whole process should take two to three months – about the same time as in the UK.

The people involved in the sales process are slightly different to the UK. You have an *abogado* (lawyer), and their role is a cut-down version of the UK solicitor. They will act in your interests, advising on the legal status of the property, conducting searches and so on. You may be more comfortable with an English *abogado*, but if so they must speak Spanish to a high standard and be familiar with Spanish property law.

The sale itself is handled by a civil servant called a *notario*. Their job is to ensure that the transfer of ownership is done fairly and properly – which is, of course, in your interests. It is quite normal for both parties to use the same *notario* – there is no conflict involved, and there is less chance of communication problems and delays. If you want your own *notario*, that is perfectly acceptable, and won't make any difference to the fees. Finally, you may also get a *gestor* (someone whose job is to deal with Spanish bureaucracy on your behalf!) to help with registering for taxes and other official matters – more on this on page 39.

There are some differences on mortgages too. The authorities in Spain are more concerned than those in the UK that people should not over-extend themselves. Spanish banks will lend you a smaller proportion of the value of the property, and take outgoings into account when calculating the maximum loan.

La propiedad y la ley – ownership and the law

Who will own your house? And what do you want to happen when the owner or one of the owners dies? These are important questions because Spanish property is subject to Spanish inheritance law, even if you live in the UK.

Under Spanish law you cannot disinherit your children – as *herederos forzosos* (reserved heirs) they are always entitled to at least a portion of it, and your spouse may also have a claim, depending on your *régimen económico matrimonial* (see below).

- 1/3 of the estate must go to any surviving children, in equal parts
- 1/3 must also go to the children, but can be divided as you wish. Your spouse has an *usufructo* (life interest) in this third.
- 1/3 can be freely disposed of.

El régimen económico matrimonial – marital ownership of property

When the *escritura* (deed of sale) is drawn up, you will be asked to specify your *régimen económico matrimonial*, which can be one of three things:

- *comunidad ganancial*: the *bienes comunes* are assets owned jointly by the couple. Property is half-owned by each spouse, so if one person dies, only half the estate needs to be disposed of; the other half remains the property of the survivor.
- *separación de bienes* (separate ownership of assets). The property will be in one person's name only, and they can disposed of it as they will, within the limitations outlined above.
- *participación* (very unusual in Spain). Each spouse has the right to participate in the earnings obtained by the other, but each administrates his/her own earnings and benefits.

El testamento – the will

These inheritance rules can create problems, especially where there are children from previous marriages. The question is, what can you do about it? Under normal circumstances, you can draw up a will dividing the estate as you please, and just stipulate that it be administered according to your own national law. However, this technically falls between two stools, because UK law says that all overseas property must be disposed of according to the law of the land, *not* UK law. Usually it is not a problem and will be respected – but if one of your offspring feels unfairly treated, they will have legal grounds to contest the will.

Private property company

You can buy a house through a company set up to own the property. The shareholders are usually members of the family or a group of friends who are buying a property together.

A company gives you more flexibility over inheritance or future ownership of the property. For example, parents can set up the company with themselves as majority shareholders, and in their wills leave sufficient shares to each other to ensure that the surviving spouse retains control of the company. If the heirs are unlikely to be able to share ownership of the property happily, it is easier to transfer shares in the company than to buy out part shares in a house. (Note that you cannot use a company to disinherit your obligatory heirs – a will which tries to do this can be declared invalid in the Spanish courts.)

Where friends want to pool their resources to buy a property, a company can be a good solution. It provides an ongoing vehicle for sharing expenses – and income if the property is rented out – and simplifies future changes of ownership, should any party later want to drop out.

Buying through a company does incur some extra costs. The company must be set up, and it must present annual accounts. If the house is solely for the owners' use, the accounts should not be a major headache, but if it is rented then the company is liable for company tax and accounting becomes more complex and costly.

You should be careful about using company structures to avoid tax. The authorities have been clamping down on this kind of loophole in recent years, and may consider your use of the property as a benefit in kind paid to you by the company – which is taxable. You will then find yourself landed with a tax bill based on the notional rental value of the property and the amount of time you have or are entitled to spend there.

Take expert advice

In all matters legal and financial, this book aims to give general guidance only. If you have any doubts or queries about what is right for you, talk to a properly qualified Spanish specialist before making any decisions.

La compra de una nueva propiedad – buying a new property

There are two main approaches to buying a new-build property. The most common way is to buy off-plan, in which you buy the house or apartment before or during building, on the basis of a plan. These usually involve a large initial payment, typically 40%, followed by stage payments until the house is completed, at which point it is officially yours.

The alternative is to have one contract which sells you the building plot and a separate contract to build the house. This gives you the security of owning the plot right from the outset – you will hear horror stories of people paying 90% of the cost of the property and then waiting for years for completion, during which time they have no legal right to anything. If you own the plot and the build goes horribly awry, you can turf the developers off your land and get someone else to finish the job.

If you can't arrange this (developers are understandably reluctant to enter into these contracts, especially on *urbanizaciones*), push for the stage payments to be linked to specific building milestones and try to include penalty clauses for late completion.

La oferta de compra – the offer to buy

Having found a resale property that you like, agreed a price with the vendor, and decided on the form of ownership, it's time to start the buying process. At the first stage, the *inmobiliaria* may ask you to sign an *oferta de compra* (offer to buy), and pay a good-faith deposit of around €1000. These are more common in commercial purchases than in domestic ones, and are more likely to be used if you have not yet agreed the price. Essentially it states that you are willing to buy the property at a given price. If the vendor accepts the offer, this proposition will be used as the basis of the contract of sale.

El contrato de compraventa – the sale contract

At this point a *contrato privado de compraventa* (private contract of sale and purchase) will be drawn up. This document does not transfer the property, but commits both you and the seller to the sale and purchase. On signing the contract you will pay *las arras* (deposit) – also called *una fianza* – of around 10%, and you will be legally bound to the sale. If you pull out now, you lose the deposit; similarly, if the seller pulls out you get double your deposit back.

This can be quite scary for us Brits, who are used to being able to change our minds right up until the last minute – but if you've ever been messed about on a house sale (as so many of us have), you will see the up-side to this arrangement!

Remember that you are still very early in the process, and you have not had surveys or searches carried out – which might bring up perfectly legitimate reasons for you to want to back out. You must make sure that the contract includes some *condiciones resolutorias* (escape clauses) which allow you to pull out without losing your deposit. There are several standard clauses which cover situations such as the following:

- unsatisfactory results from surveys or searches
- lack of planning permission for expected building work
- your failure to secure a mortgage
- the seller's failure to clear existing debts on the property – in Spain, mortgages are attached to a property, not to the person, and it is possible to inherit someone else's debt if you're not careful!

Be as specific as possible on your conditions – make it a specific mortgage at a specific rate, otherwise the seller can insist that you proceed with the sale on the grounds that there are other mortgages available, even if they're not good value for you. Your *abogado* will help you draw up sufficient clauses to give you a reasonable way out if you need it.

The contract must also contain the following information:

- Description of the property, its dimensions and related costs. Where appropriate, it should clearly identify the *zonas comunes* (communal areas) and *gastos de comunidad* (service charges).
- Details of the *notario* and the buying and selling parties, including your *régimen matrimonial* if appropriate.
- The price and date of payments. For stage payments on new-build properties, building milestones and penalties for late completion should also be specified if possible.
- The amount of the deposit.
- If you will be taking out a *hipoteca* (mortgage), how much you are borrowing and where you hope to borrow from.
- A date for signing the deed of sale.

The property is now taken off the market. The deposit must be in Euros, and if you do not yet have a Spanish bank account, you may not be able to make immediate payment. This should not be a problem. You can agree to pay within a set time, paying by bank transfer once you get back to the UK.

Between now and the signing of the *escritura* (deed of sale) which officially transfers ownership to you, your *abogado* will conduct the necessary checks and searches, and you will need to arrange finances. You will also need to pop down to the local police station or *Oficina de Extranjeros* (Office for Foreigners) to get yourself an NIE – *Número de Identificación de Extranjeros* (ID number for foreign nationals), which you will need for tax purposes. You can find a list of *Oficinas de Extranjeros* on the web: **www.mir.es/extranje/extdonde.htm**. It's a good idea to open a Spanish bank account too, to make it easier to pay bills by *domiciliación bancaria* (direct debit).

Documentation

You should see copies of various documents from the seller before signing the contract, depending on whether the property is a new build or resale.

For new build properties

- *certificado de fin de obra* – confirmation that the building work is complete.
- *cédula de habitación* – a document from the *ayuntamiento* (town hall) certifying that the property is fit for habitation.
- the *cédula* may be contingent on other documents such as a *boletín de instalaciones eléctricas* from a registered electrician to say that the electrical work is safe.

For resale properties

- their *escritura* and *nota simple* (land registry record) to prove the seller's ownership and to establish whether there are any debts attached to the property.
- passport or *certificado de residencia*/NIE (ID for foreigners) to prove their identity.
- *certificado de empadronamiento* – a document from the *ayuntamiento* showing who lives at the property.
- recent bills for utilities and service charges.

Can your Spanish cope?

You need good Spanish to be able to cope with the legal and technical terminology in the contract and related documents. If you have any doubts about your ability to fully understand the documents, ask for copies, take them away and get them translated. Take advice from an English-speaking *abogado* or a UK solicitor who understands Spanish property law. Don't sign anything lightly.

Lexicon: el contrato – the contract

abogado (m)	solicitor/lawyer
boletín (m) de instalaciones eléctricas	certificate of electrical safety
cédula de habitación (f)	certificate to prove house is habitable
cláusula penal (f)	penalty clause

compra (m)	purchase
comprador (m), compradora (f)	purchaser
comunidad (f) de bienes	marital co-ownership of assets
condiciones resolutorias	conditions to be met for the agreement to be valid
contrato (m) privado de compraventa	contract of sale
escritura (f)	deed of sale
gastos (mpl) de comunidad	service charges
gestor (m)	middleman for dealing with bureaucracy
herederos forzosos (mpl)	obligatory heirs, who must receive a part of the estate
hipoteca (f)	mortgage
informe urbanístico (m)	town planning search
nota simple (f)	land registry entry
notario (m)	lawyer and public official
oferta de compra (f)	offer to buy, at a stated price – this is not a contract
oferta de venta (f)	offer to sell at a stated price – again, this not a contract
régimen económico matrimonial (m)	marital property ownership arrangements
separación (f) de bienes	separate marital ownership of assets
vendedor (m), vendedora (f)	seller
venta (f)	sale
zonas comunes (fpl)	communal areas

Finance

Before the sale can be completed, the purchase money must be transferred. There are three main ways to do this:

- Transfer cash from your UK bank account, **in Euros**, using Swift interbank transfer. You will need to know the recipient's bank and his IBAN (International Bank Account

Number) to do this. The money should take around five days to get there, but may take longer. If you are in a hurry, your bank can do a so-called 'same day' Swift transfer, and that should only take a couple of days. Our experience is that banks are not to be relied on for prompt transfers. Give yourself plenty of time, and check that the money has arrived.

- Obtain from your UK bank a banker's draft, which guarantees payment, in Euros, and give this to the *notario*.
- Open a bank account in Spain, transfer the necessary funds into it and give the *notario* a Spanish cheque. You will have to have a Spanish bank account if you take out a Spanish mortgage, but it will in any case make your continuing life there much simpler. With a Spanish account you can set up direct debits to pay the tax and utility bills and save a lot of trouble – being out of the country at the time is not an acceptable excuse for not paying a bill when it is due! It takes minutes to open a Spanish bank account. All you need is your passport and proof of your (intended) address in Spain – you don't even need to put in any money. They will happily arrange to send your correspondence to your UK address if required.

Mortgages

Spanish mortgage lenders usually require a deposit of 20 to 25% of the purchase price. Interest rates are currently lower than in the UK, and are usually fixed; a repayment mortgage is the norm. Don't count on rental income to pay your mortgage either – lenders will not usually take possible rental income into account when calculating how much they'll lend you. Buy-to-let deals are very uncommon, though some lenders may consider it in solid rental areas.

Spanish banks are more cautious in their lending than those in the UK. You cannot normally borrow more than four times your total income. More to the point, you cannot normally borrow so much that your total debt ratio – outgoings, including other loan repayments, compared to net income – is higher than 33%. If your income is high or you want to borrow a small percentage of the property's value, then the bank may allow a higher ratio.

Do you have the cash?

The mortgage can only cover property, not the legal costs of buying (up to 10% or more, see pages 37–8), so you must have the cash for these too. For example, with a €100,000 house you would need at least €20,000 for the deposit and €10,000 for the fees and taxes. With all the other inevitable costs of moving and settling, you would be ill-advised to start out on the venture without at least €40,000 to hand.

If you take out a Spanish mortgage, do bear in mind that not only do interest rates vary, exchange rates also vary. A 25-year €100,000 mortgage now costs around £4,000 p.a. An increase of 1% in the interest rate would increase it by a little over £400. A fall in the exchange rate from €1.45 to the pound to €1.3 would cost about the same. If you're a friend of George Soros, ask him what he thinks the exchange and interest rates will do – if not, don't borrow too close to your limits!

If you have plenty of equity in your UK house, you could remortgage it to release funds for an outright purchase in Spain. If you do this, you must organise the remortgage before signing the initial contract, or have a *condición resolutoria* written into it to cover the possibility of the remortgage not going through. The sale cannot be cancelled without losing your deposit if a remortgage is not obtained.

Whatever you do, take good advice and compare costs.

La escritura – the deed of sale

This is the document that transfers ownership. In drawing it up, the *notario* will have checked the vendor's right to sell, the boundaries of the property and any rights of way or restrictions on it. You will have been asked for a copy of your birth certificate, and if you are married, you will have had to confirm your marital status and your *régimen matrimonial* so that ownership of the property is clear.

You should get a draft copy of the *escritura* some time before the transfer day. This will give you a chance to have it translated and checked, if necessary, by a competent professional, and to raise any queries you may have.

You will get to keep an unsigned copy of the final *escritura*, known as the *copia simple*. The original document goes to the authorities to be stamped and signed in various places to make it all official. It then becomes a public document known as the *escritura pública* (public deed) or *registro de propiedad* (property registration). You can take a copy of this too if you like, but the *copia simple* is enough for any legal purposes to prove your ownership of the property.

> **El poder – power of attorney**
>
> **If it is not convenient for you to go – perhaps at very short notice – to the *notario*'s office to sign the contract, you can give someone a power of attorney to sign for you. The document to set up the power of attorney must comply with Spanish requirements, but is then signed before a notary public in the UK, to be authenticated. Some UK agents will suggest you give them power of attorney to save you the cost of another trip to Spain – it's all above board, but only do it if you feel you can trust them.**

Fees and charges

Notarios perform a public function, and their fees are set by the state, on a sliding scale according to the value of the property. They are non-negotiable, and there's no point in trying to shop around for a cheaper alternative. Transfer tax or stamp duty, registration costs and other official charges are also paid via the *notario*, so the total bill can be significant.

The fees and charges depend partly on whether you are buying a new build or resale property.

New build

- 0.5% Stamp duty
- 7% *IVA – Impuesto sobre el Valor Añadido* (VAT)

Resale

- 6% or 7% *impuesto sobre transmisiones patrimoniales* (transfer tax – it varies between regions)
- *plusvalía* (capital gains tax) – see page 39.

Costs common to all purchases

- *notarios*' fees are fixed amounts which increase with the value of the property, but work out at about 0.5%
- 0.5% *registro de propiedad* (land registry fees)
- 1% lawyer's fees

Property taxes

There are five property taxes, not all of which may apply.

IBI – impuesto sobre bienes inmuebles (property tax)

This is a local tax that is paid by the owner of the house at the beginning of every year. It is normal practice for the buyer to reimburse the seller for the tax for the remaining portion of the year.

The tax is based on the property's rentable value (*valor catastral*) and set by the local town hall. The level currently ranges from 0.4% to 1.1%. If you buy a ruin and restore it to its former glory and beyond, the *IBI* will go up accordingly.

Other local taxes

Municipal authorities will also charge various taxes to cover local services such as *basura* (rubbish collection). Together with the *IBI*, these shouldn't set you back more than about €500 a year for a decent-sized house.

Patrimonio (wealth tax)

This is charged on a sliding scale based on the net value of your property assets – i.e. the house value minus any outstanding mortgage. At the time of writing, it starts at 0.2% for amounts less than €167,129, rising to 2.5% for anything over €10.7m.

Impuesto sobre transmisiones patrimoniales (transfer tax)

Tax due on the sale of any residential property, and calculated on its declared price. This is not necessarily the amount paid. Buyers and sellers sometimes agree to make the declared price less than the actual amount paid, to reduce the tax. We would advise against taking part in any such deal.

Impuesto de plusvalía (capital gains tax)

This is another local tax with varying rates, and is based upon the increase in the value of the *land* rather than on the property, and will be higher the longer that you have owned it. In theory this is payable by the vendor, but since the bill only arrives long after the sale has gone through, the convention is that the buyer pays it. Usually a corresponding amount is knocked off the price of the property – contact the *ayuntamiento* to get an estimate of the *plusvalía* – and negotiate accordingly.

There is also a capital gains tax for non-residents, currently set at 18% of the difference between the buying and selling prices.

El gestor – the bureaucratic go-between

In Spain there is a whole trade which does not exist in the UK – the *gestor* is a professional middleman whose sole function is to deal with bureaucracy for others. This is not something which has sprung up to service foreign residents; Spaniards regularly use them for routine tasks like renewing a parking permit, simply because of the time you can waste standing in queues or being shunted from pillar to post. If you deal with the grey machine yourself, you'll save yourself a bit of money – but will probably realise quite quickly why people do use a *gestor* if they can possibly afford to!

Lexicon: la venta – the sale

copia simple (f)	certificate of purchase
domiciliación bancaria (f)	direct debit
escritura (f)	deed of sale
IBI – Impuesto sobre Bienes Inmuebles (m)	local property tax
nota simple (f)	document showing ownership and debts of a property
patrimonio (m)	wealth tax
plusvalía (f)	capital gains tax
registro catastral (m)	local register of land holdings
registro (m) de propiedad	registration of ownership

Los servicios – services

Utilities in Spain are all supplied by a mixture of private and state-owned companies. The services are mostly good in towns and *urbanizaciones*, and slightly more erratic in rural areas. Costs are comparable to or cheaper than in the UK, apart from water, but do check your first few bills carefully – there are reports of overcharging.

The utilities that are already connected to your house should be transferred to your name by the *inmobiliaria* or *notario* handling the sale. If they don't provide this service for you, contact the vendor and get the details of their contracts. It should be simple enough to have the contracts transferred to your name at the appropriate time. Getting connected to mains water, electricity, gas or telephone for the first time may be a bit more involved and take a little longer to achieve. If your property is on an *urbanización*, connection to services should be arranged for you, and the cost included in the sale – developers should not charge you extra for this.

Electricity is supplied by four companies and on a wide range of tariffs, which depend primarily on how much power you need to have on tap. You choose the level of supply, from 3kW to 36kW, to match your possible peak demands. You can run the normal range of lights, TV, washing machine and other appliances on a 9kW supply, increasing to 12 or 15kW if you have high demand appliances such as an electric oven or heating system. Connection costs vary from €100 to €300 depending on location.

The electrical supply is 220 volts in most of Spain, though there are some areas where it is 110 volts. Bills are sent out every two months, and you can pay by *domiciliación bancaria* (direct debit) to avoid disconnection for missed payments. Alternatively, if you give the supplier your address in the UK they will send your bills there.

Gas is only piped to houses in larger towns, so you will quite probably use *bombonas de gas* (bottled butane) for your gas heating and cooking needs. These are cheap, last a decent amount of time and are widely available at garages and elsewhere. You can also arrange a contract with Repsol Butano to get them delivered to your door, which is handy – they're very heavy! Also,

Repsol Butano will carry out a safety inspection on your gas appliances prior to agreeing the contract.

Water is usually metered, and the costs rise sharply the more water you use. It may cost as little as 50 cents per cubic metre for low-level consumption, but as your monthly quota rises, so the cost per unit rises, and you can soon find that your swimming pool is costing you a fortune to keep full, especially in dry rural areas. Some *urbanizaciones* offer unlimited water supply deals – you will usually pay for the privilege, but at least you know up front what your bills are going to look like.

If your house is connected to the *alcantarillado* (mains drains), there will be an additional charge for waste water.

If you need a landline telephone, talk to Telefónica. It currently costs about €15 a month for a standard line, including installation and a handset. They also do reasonable Internet offers, such as broadband for €10 a month plus €77 for modem and installation.

In towns, *la basura* (rubbish) is collected from in front of your house every night except Sundays. Ask your neighbours what time you should put it out – there are sometimes fines for putting it out too early (it's a hot country, so smelly rubbish can be a real issue). *Urbanizaciones* generally have large communal bins and ask you to take your rubbish there in sealed bags. In the countryside you must take your rubbish to the municipal bins, which may be some distance away.

Reciclaje (recycling) provision has been historically non-existent, but is on the rise now, and the Spanish recycle more than we do in the UK. There will be collection bins for paper, cans and bottles near you, though doorstep recycling services are not so common.

Ask at the *ayuntamiento* about collection of large waste items, or to locate your nearest waste disposal site.

Lexicon: los servicios – services

agua (f)	water
alcantarillado (m)	mains drains
ayuntamiento (m)	town hall

basura (f)	rubbish
bombona (f) de gas	bottle of butane
electricidad (f)	electricity
gas (m)	gas
reciclaje (m)	recycling
teléfono (m)	telephone

English–Spanish quick reference

The initial contract – el contrato privado de compraventa

agreement to buy	oferta (f) de comprar
conditional clauses	condiciones resolutorias (fpl)
contract of sale	contrato (m) privado de compraventa
co-ownership, marital	comunidad (f) de bienes
mortgage	hipoteca (f)
notary	notario (m)
penalty clause	cláusula penal (f)
purchase	compra (f)
purchaser	comprador (m)/compradora (f)
reserved heirs	herederos forzosos (mpl)
seller	vendedor (m)/vendedora (f)
town planning search	informe urbanístico (m)

The sale – la venta

capital gains	(impuesto de) plusvalía (f)
certificate of purchase	copia simple (f)
deed of transfer	escritura (f)
land ownership document	nota simple (f)
land register	registro catastral (m)
property tax	IBI – Impuesto sobre Bienes Inmuebles

registration of ownership	registro (m) de propiedad
VAT	IVA – Impuesto sobre el Valor Añadido
wealth tax	patrimonio (m)

Services – los servicios

bottle of butane	bombona (f) de gas
electricity	electricidad (f)
gas	gas (m)
mains drains	alcantarillado (m)
recycling	reciclaje (m)
rubbish	basura (f)
telephone	teléfono (m)
telephone line	línea (f) de teléfono
town hall	ayuntamiento (m)
water	agua (m)

03 las obras – building work

Almost the same...

The Spanish have planning permission and building regulations the same as we do in the UK, only more so. They control what can be built, where, its size, style and sometimes even its colour. By and large, it's a good idea. The controls help to preserve regional identities, to create more harmonious townscapes and to avoid blots on the countryside. It's a bit of a shame they weren't more forcefully applied back in the days when ugly concrete high-rises were thrown up along the coast!

There are different levels of control:

- If you are going to build a new house, extend an existing one outwards or upwards, add a garage or a substantial outbuilding, you will need a *licencia de obra mayor* (building permit for major works). To obtain one of these, you must employ an *arquitecto* (architect) to draw up proper plans to support your application.
- If your changes are structural but fairly minor – like moving a partition wall or swapping the kitchen and bathroom around – you will need a *licencia de obra menor* (building permit for minor works).

As in the UK, all building work is subject to local and national planning regulations, and health and safety rules.

Check at the ayuntamiento (town hall)

The *ayuntamiento* is central to all this. It's where the planning permits are issued, and it's where you will find list of registered tradesmen. It can take a longer or shorter time to get permissions agreed, and there can be more or fewer nits picked in the process. Much of this liaison will be done by your *arquitecto* for larger works, and you might work through a *gestor* even for smaller jobs. However, if you turn up in person at the beginning at the process and show that you want to be part of their community, it could make things go more smoothly. It's amazing how much goodwill a few words of broken Spanish can get you!

Building and planning regulations vary from place to place, so try to arrange to discuss your plans with someone at the *ayuntamiento*, or with a local architect or builder. They will be able to give you a clear idea of what kind of permission is required and what you will need to do to get it.

PGOU – the town planning brief

Almost all municipalities have a *PGOU (Plan General de Ordenación Urbana)* – a map and a planning brief that determines what use can be made of the land. If you're buying a plot of land, these are the main land use categories it might fall into:

- *Terreno rústico* – agricultural land. If there is an existing farmhouse on the land, there will probably be permission to renovate it, but don't expect to be allowed to add a dozen holiday cottages and start renting them out!
- *Terreno urbanizable* – land designated for development. Your proposed building works will still be subject to strict planning controls, and you will of course need to submit detailed plans before you start building – but in principle you should be able to build here.
- *Terreno industrial* – land set aside for industrial or commercial use – check for specific restrictions before assuming you can open an asbestos factory…

Wherever you are buying, it's as well to check that any future developments won't alter the character of the neighbourhood. The *PGOU* is usually updated every four years, but will probably not change radically from one version to the next except in areas of very rapid expansion.

Ask at the *ayuntamiento* to see the *PGOU*. They should be happy to show it to you.

Licencia de obra mayor – planning permission

The first step in getting a *licencia* is to pick up a form from the *ayuntamiento*. There are several varieties of these, depending on whether you are doing minor or major works, building a new house or extending an existing one.

The forms are quite complicated (now you see why some people employ a *gestor*!) and should be accompanied by supporting documents.

You will normally have to supply:

- a map showing the land's boundaries and access roads;
- detailed architect's drawings and plans;
- a description of the materials to be used;
- photo-montage or sketch artist's impression of the finished job, giving both a close-up and distant view of site.

The building must conform to regulations over the ratio of house to land area, the height and pitch of the roof, the position of windows in relation to neighbouring properties, and assorted other factors. As a rule of thumb, if your building will look basically the same as its neighbours, then it will conform.

The *PGOU* sets out any special requirements in your area, e.g. the minimum distance from the house to the boundary of the land or restrictions on the type of construction or roofing material.

The local council's architect will go through the application and may request some alterations. These must be accepted and acted on. Do not assume anything about the state of the application if you still haven't heard anything several weeks later. The wheels of Spanish bureaucracy can turn very slowly and you may need to chase the matter up from time to time. Don't give up and start work anyway though – if permission is not granted, they can make you undo the work at your own cost.

Licencia de obra menor – permission for minor work

This is a slightly simpler form, but must again be accompanied by plans of the site and of the building, and drawings or photo-montages to illustrate the end result. In some cases, a brief sketch and description of the work may be sufficient.

Los obreros – the builders

El arquitecto – the architect

A Spanish architect often doubles as project manager for the building work too – he or she will draw up plans, deal with the paperwork, find tradesmen, get estimates and oversee the work for you. There is no real equivalent in the UK – the nearest is the project manager that you might find on larger sites, or the small master builder who will bring in other trades as they are needed.

A good *arquitecto* should be able to draw on a wide knowledge of materials and techniques to suggest solutions that you would never have thought of yourself. If you want to have the work done while you are in the UK, then employing an *arquitecto* is an obvious solution even for the simpler jobs. Even if you are there yourself, employing an *arquitecto* should ensure that the job is done better, and the extra cost may not be that much in the long run.

The informal quality checks work as well, or better, in Spain as in the UK especially in the rural areas. Tradesmen prefer to work in their local area, and to rely more on word of mouth than advertising for their business, so reputation is important. Ask your neighbours, or your vendors or the *inmobiliaria* if they can recommend people for the work.

Keep an eye out for the names of builders on the notices where building is in progress. And if all else fails, Spain has *Páginas Amarillas* (Yellow Pages) just as we do.

DIY at your own risk!

If you do the work yourself or have it done on informally, 'cash in hand', it will not be guaranteed, and you could have problems if you sell the house in the next few years.

Other trades

- *contratista de obras* – building contractor
- *albañil* – bricklayer
- *enyesador* – plasterer
- *carpintero de armar* – carpenter, specialising in large work such as roof timbers
- *carpintero* – joiner, for windows, doors, etc.
- *fontanero* – plumber
- *electricista* – electrician

We will meet these and other tradesmen in the rest of the book.

El presupuesto – the estimate

When you have found your tradesman ask for a *presupuesto* (estimate). You should not have to pay for this; most will offer a *presupuesto gratis* (free estimate).

The *presupuesto* sets the price and the specifications, and will be the finished price for the job – unless you change the specifications later. But do be clear about what you are asking for. There have been cases of people getting a *presupuesto* for a bathroom to find that it only included equipment and delivery. Make sure that *instalación* (installation) is included in the *presupuesto*!

Estimates and budgets

***Presupuesto* also means 'budget', so when you have decided what you want, get several firms to give you a *presupuesto* (estimate) for the work, and see which best matches your, um... *presupuesto* (budget).**

Lexicon: las obras – building work

alcalde (m)	mayor
arquitecto (m)	architect and project manager
artesano (m)	tradesman
contratista (m) de obras	building contractor
formulario (m)	form
licencia (f) de obra...	planning permission...
...mayor	...for major works
...menor	...for minor works
obrero (m)	workman
PGOU (Plan General de Ordenación Urbana)	town planning brief
presupuesto (m)	estimate
presupuesto gratis (m)	free estimate
solar (m)	building site/building plot

English–Spanish quick reference

architect	arquitecto (m)
building contractor	contratista (m) de obras
building site	solar (m)
estimate	presupuesto (m)
form	formulario (m)
mayor	alcalde (m)
planning permission...	licencia (f) de obra...
...major	...mayor
... minor	...menor
town planning brief	PGOU (Plan General de Ordenación Urbana)
tradesman	artesano (m)
workman	obrero (m)

04 la estructura – the structure

Almost the same...

Outside of the major tourist areas – i.e. anywhere more than a few miles inland from the coast – the Spanish are very keen on preserving their cultural history. We have listed buildings and preservation areas in the UK, and so do the Spanish. But they go further. They believe that, though the house may belong to you, its external appearance is a matter of common concern. If you plan to build a new house, or change an existing one, and want yours to stand out from its neighbours, think again. You can have your individuality, but within the limits of the regional look.

The ornate stonework and wrought-iron balconies of grand old apartments in cities like Madrid and Barcelona will be protected, and you won't be able to slap an asphalt roof in amongst the terracotta tiles in a village in the interior, or paint the walls blue when everyone else's are neatly whitewashed. Some things you won't want to change anyway – if you buy an old *cortijo*, why would you knock down that cool shady courtyard in the middle of the house, or trade its Moorish arches for aluminium joists?

The majority of British house purchases in Spain are in *urbanizaciones*. The appearance of these ranges from simple whitewashed apartments and terraced houses, to groups of extravagant villas with huge French windows looking out over private pools set about with arches and waterfalls. On a purely practical level, all old Spanish houses – and some new ones – have solid walls. Cavity walls are not standard, as they are in the UK, though they may sometimes be found in colder areas. The walls of new houses are often built of hollow red bricks, which are large and light and go up very quickly. With rendering on the outside and insulated plasterboard on the inside, these have reasonable insulating qualities. Breeze blocks are also quite common, and offer better insulation.

Check at the ayuntamiento

- If you are planning any structural change to the house, either external *or* internal, talk to the planning officer at the *ayuntamiento* at an early stage – see Chapter 3.
- The *ayuntamiento* should have a list of registered tradesmen in your area.

La estructura – the structure

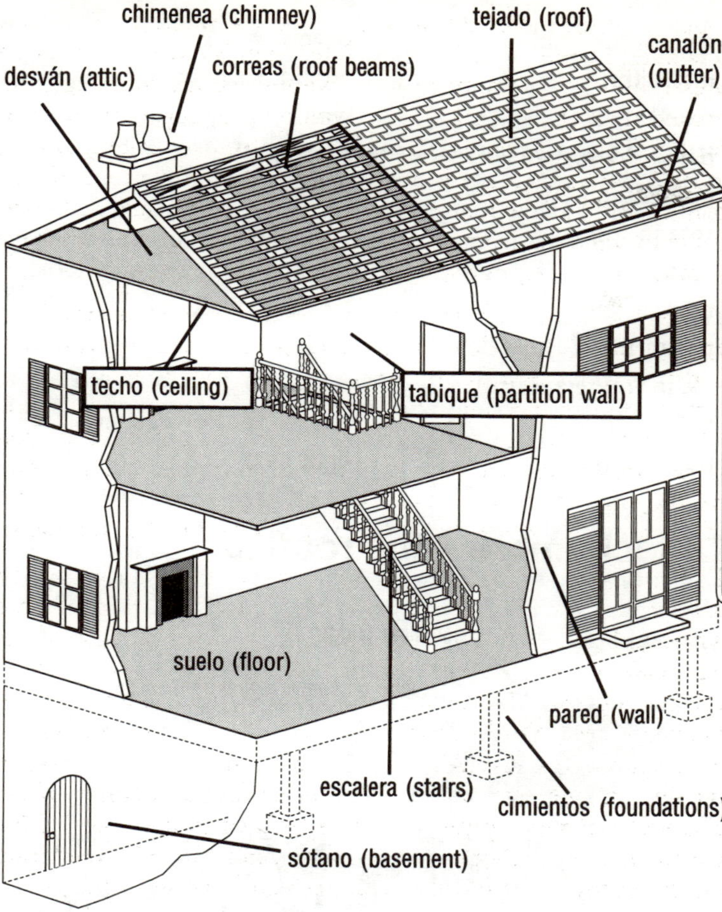

ático (m)	top floor apartment – usually with full or partial terrace roof
carcoma (f)	woodworm
chimenea (f)	chimney, fireplace
cimientos (mpl)	foundations
claraboya (f)	skylight
correas (fpl)	roof beams
cubierta inclinada (m)	sloping roof
desperdicios (mpl)	rubbish

desván (m)	attic/loft
escalera (f)	stairs
escombros (mpl)	rubble
moho (m)	mould, mildew
pared (f)	wall
pared divisoria/medianera (f)	party wall
podredumbre (f)	rot
sótano (m)	basement
suelo (m)	floor
tabique (m)	partition wall
techo (m)	ceiling
techo (m)/tejado (m)	roof
terraza (f)	terrace roof or balcony
tragaluz (m)	light shaft

La techumbre – the roofing

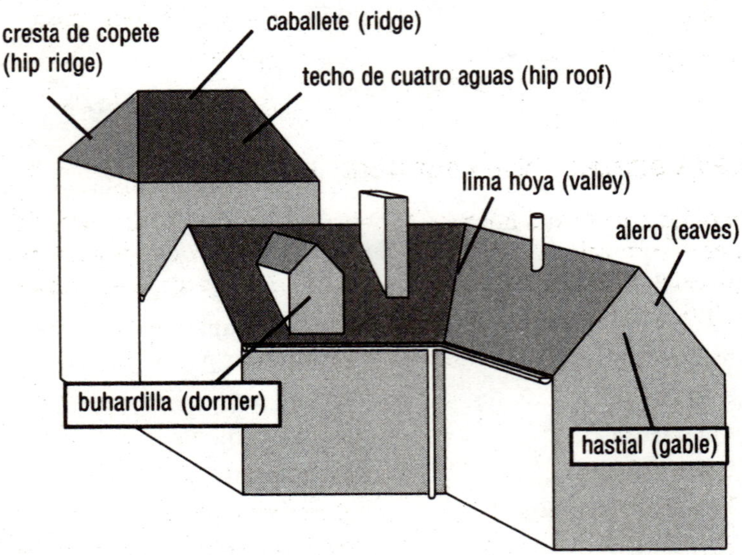

alero (m)	eaves
azotea	terrace roof
banda para junta (f)	flashing
...de plomo/de zinc	...of lead/of zinc
buhardilla (f)	attic room
buhardilla (f) ventana	dormer window
caballete (m)	ridge
canalón (m)	gutter
cartón alquitranado para techumbres	lining felt
cresta (f) de copete	hip ridge
cubierta (f) a cuatro aguas	hip roof
fachada (f) de alero	eaves board or fascia
faldón	sloping section of roof
frontón (m)	pediment
hastial	gable end
lima (f) hoya	valley (inner angle where two roofs meet)
lima (f) tesa	outer angle where roofs meet
tragaluz (m)	(Velux) skylight

tragaluz (skylight)

Las correas – the roof beams

In older houses and house with gables, the roof will normally be made from rafters on a ridge beam and wall plates, braced by horizontal beams. In other cases, ready-made triangular trusses will be used to create the basic structure.

armadura (f)	roof truss
desván (m)	attic
bóveda (f)	roof arch
buhardilla (f)	attic room
buhardilla ventana (f)	dormer window
carrera (f)	roof plate, rests on top of walls
correa (f)	horizontal beam
correa intermedia (f)	purlin, horizontal tie on rafters

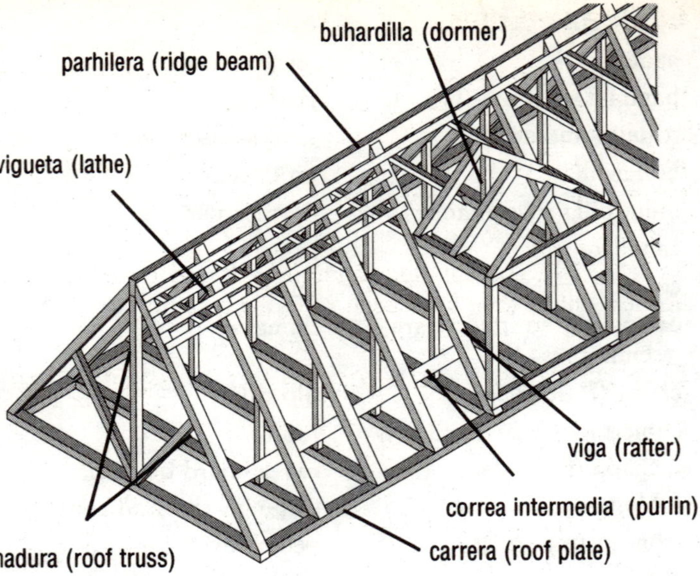

listón (m)	batten
montado (m)	vertical beam
parhilera (f)	ridge beam
pino (m)	pine
preservador (m) de madera	wood preservative
roble (m)	oak
varilla (f)	lathe
viga (f)	beam, rafter
vigueta (f)	lathe

An attic with *bóvedas* (arches), like this one, will be easier to convert into a habitable room, than one where the roof is formed from trusses

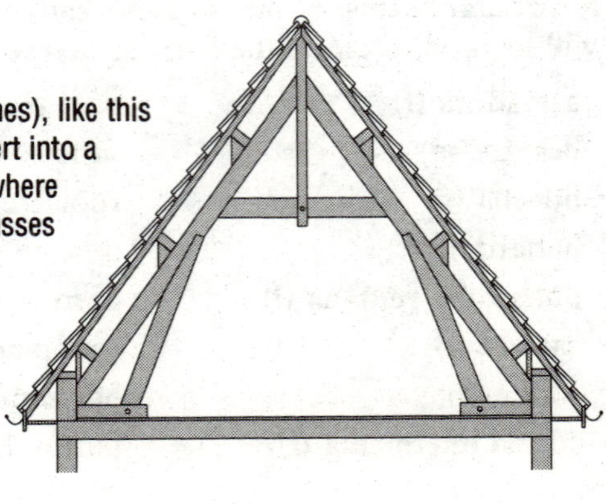

Lathes and tiles

If the roof is to be covered with slates of flat tiles, these will be hung on lathes. Lathes are also used now with curved tiles, but on older houses you may find flat planking or triangular supports. The tiles are sometimes simply placed on top of these – not attached – and have a tendency to slip steadily down the roof over the years.

As in the UK, you will not find lining felt under the tiles of older houses, unless they have been reroofed recently.

Los materiales para tejado – roofing materials

teja curva
(curved tile)

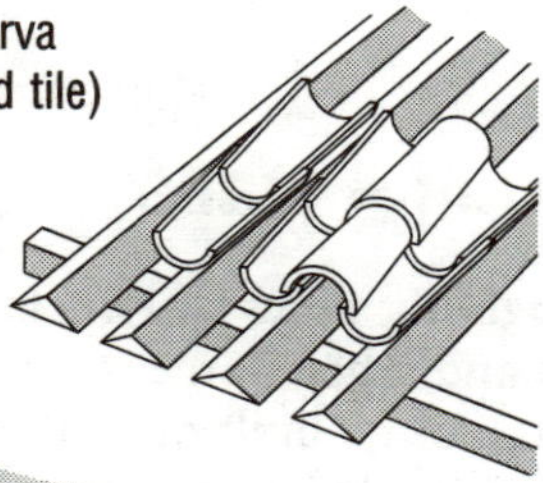

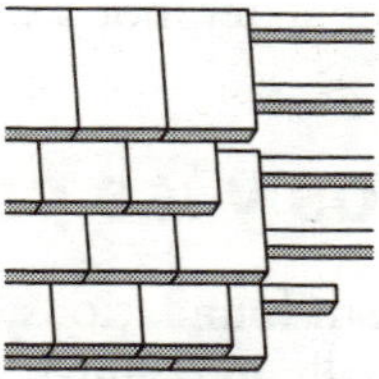

teja llana
(flat tile)

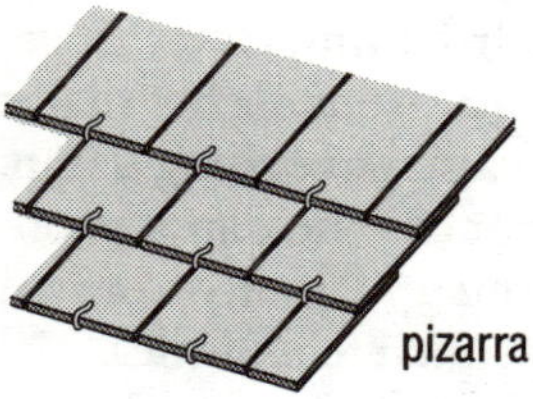

pizarra (slate)

tejado de paja (thatch)

barro cocido (m)	clay
cartón alquitranado para techumbre (m)	roofing felt
clavo (m) para pizarra	slate nail
pizarra (f)	slate
teja (f)	tile
teja curva/romana (f)	curved tile
teja plana (f)	flat tile
tejado de paja (m)	thatched roof – literally 'roof of straw'

Which word?

Sometimes there are several words for the same thing. Try to learn one well enough to be able to ask for it, and others well enough to recognise them when you hear them.

Roofing tradesmen

- If you want to build, adapt or mend the roofing timbers, you need *un carpintero de armar* – one who works with unfinished structural timbers.
- If you need to replace or mend a roof, you need *un tejador* (a roofer). And if it's a slate roof, make sure that he is *un pizarrero* (a slater, not a pizza delivery boy!).

Los muros y las paredes – walls

Walls start from foundations, though not necessarily… In older houses, especially in country areas and where large stones were the building material, the walls were often built directly on the ground. Two possible problems can arise from this. You can get subsidence, though with an old house it's a reasonable bet that it has sunk as much as it's going to. You may also have rising damp, as there will be no barrier beneath the stones. The damp problem will be worse if the original – breathing – floor of beaten earth or flagstones has been replaced by concrete and tiles.

If a wall is outside, it is called *un muro*; inside it is called *una pared* – even if you're talking about two sides of the same stones.

Los cimientos – foundations

aislante hidrófugo (m)	damp course
albañilería (f)	masonry/bricklaying
cimientos (mpl)	foundations
excavaciones (fpl)	excavation
grava (f)	hardcore
grieta (f)	crack!
rejuntar los muros	point – renew mortar of walls

humedad (f)	damp
humedad (f) de paredes	rising damp
muro (m)	wall (external)
pared (f)	wall (internal)
zanja (f)	trench
zapata (f)	footing

External walls

For new building, the Spanish favour *ladrillos huecos* (hollow concrete or clay blocks). These come in a wide range of sizes and cross-sections, offering different weight to strength ratios. The resulting walls are not very attractive when bare, but they are not intended to remain bare. The outside is normally rendered with mortar and whitewashed. The inside is rendered or lined with *paneles de yeso* (plasterboard).

Where a wall is built with a cavity, the structure is usually different from that in the UK. Here a cavity wall has an inner load-bearing skin of brick or breeze block, and an outer skin of brick. In Spain the cavity is formed by adding a thin inner skin to a standard thickness, load-bearing outer wall. Both inner and outer walls are often made of hollow bricks.

Instant walls!

If you want a very strong, solid wall quickly, use the hollowest bricks – the ones with really big holes through them – to build a dry wall, slide reinforcing rods down through the holes, then fill with wet concrete.

Los tabiques – partition walls

Some or all of the internal walls of a house will be *tabiques* (partitions). Smaller farms and terraced houses or apartments in towns are often built with the floor and ceiling joists supported solely by the outside walls. Keep this in mind when you look around old houses. *Tabiques* are easily removed and rebuilt elsewhere if you want to remodel the internal layout.

Some wall styles

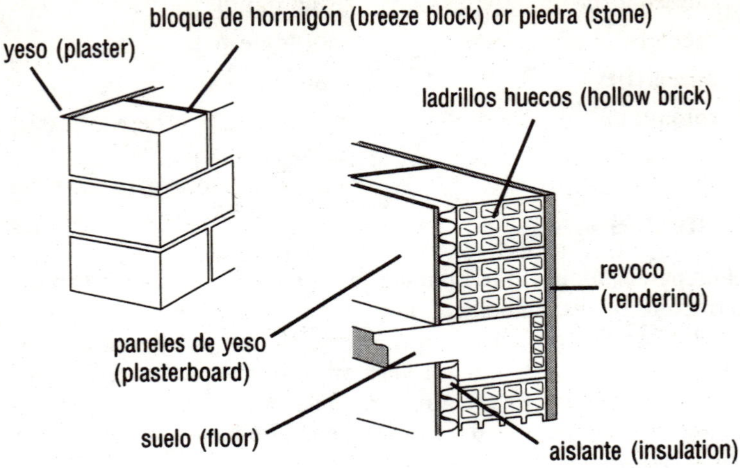

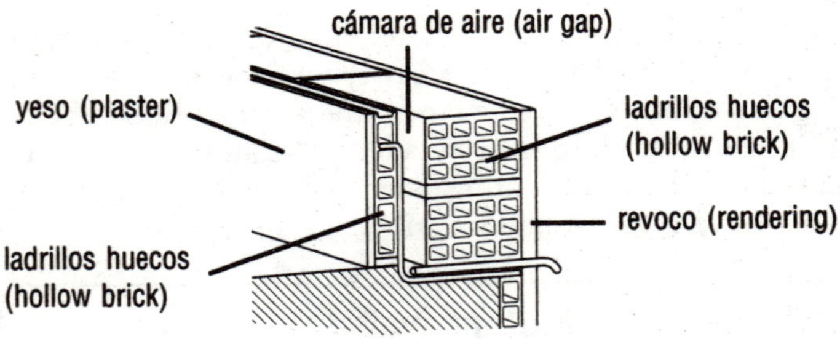

Old *tabiques* are likely to be lathe and plaster or single-skin brick. New ones are quickly built from thin hollow bricks, plasterboard on wooden frames or plaster blocks.

Digression: bloques de yeso – plaster blocks

You won't find these in the UK, but plaster blocks are worth investigating. They are typically 66 × 50 cm, in widths from 7 to 12 cm and come in different weights and finishes – including waterproof ones for bathrooms and lightweight ones for loft conversions. They are assembled like brickwork – but much easier and faster – need no framework and can be cut with a wood saw. Exposed corners can be reinforced with an angled metal strip, if required. After a little fine filling of the ends and joints, the new wall is ready for decorating.

Wall materials

aislante (m)	insulation
anclaje de muro (m)	wall tie
arena (f)	sand
bloque (m) de hormigón	breeze block – these come in solid concrete with large moulded gaps, or in the more common UK form (celular)
bloque (m) de yeso	plaster block
cal (f)	lime
cámara (f) de aire	air gap – may contain insulation
cemento (m)	cement
de armazón de madera	half-timbered
dintel (m)	lintel
enlucido (m)	lining – could be plasterboard
granito (m)	granite
gravilla (f)	coarse sand
hormigón (m)	concrete
hormigón armado (m)	reinforced concrete
ladrillo (m)	brick
ladrillo hueco (m)	hollow brick
ladrillo refractario (m)	firebrick
mármol (m)	marble
mortero bastardo (m)	mixed lime/cement mortar
mortero de cal (m)	lime mortar
mortero de cemento (m)	cement mortar
panel (m)/tablero (m)	panel
panel (m) de escayola	plasterboard
panel (m) de yeso	plasterboard
piedra (f)	stone
piedra arenisca (f)	sandstone
piedra caliza (f)	limestone
piedra de cantera (f)	quarry stone

piedra labrada (f)	dressed stone
revoco (m)	rendering (external)
tablero aglomerado (m)	chipboard panel
tapajuntas metálico (m)	angled strip for reinforcing corner of plaster wall
zarzo (m)	wattle and daub – a mixture of clay, straw and other substances on a framework of woven sticks

Aislamiento – insulation

acristalamiento doble (m)	double glazing
burlete (m) de espuma	foam strip
corcho granulado (m)	cork particles
fibra (f) de vidrio	fibreglass
guarnecido (m)	draught-proofing
junta de silicona (f)	rubber beading
lana de roca (f)	rockwool
panel aislante (m)	insulation panel
panel compuesto (m)	composite panel – e.g. plasterboard backed with an insulating material
panel sandwich (m)	insulating material between two layers of plasterboard
poliestireno (m)	polystyrene
poliuretano (m)	polyurethane
vermiculita (f)	mica particles
vidrio compuesto/doble (m)	double-panelled window glass
vidrio con cámara de aire (m)	double-panelled window glass

Building tradesmen

- A builder is *un albañil*, whether he's a general builder, a brick-layer or a stonemason.
- For plastering, you need *un enyesador*.

Las herramientas de albañil – builder's tools

Brickwork

pala (shovel)

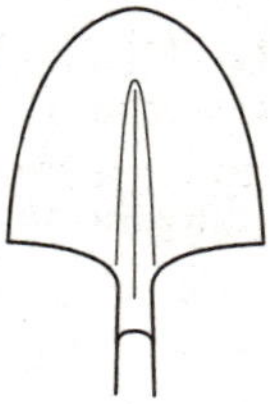

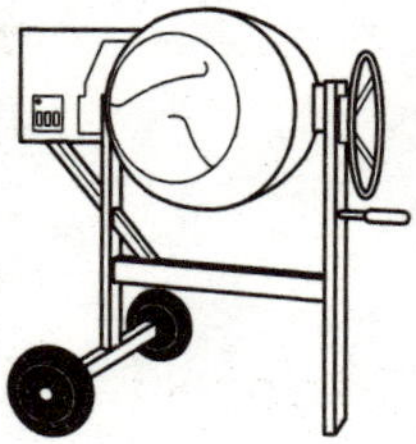

hormigonera
(concrete mixer)

paleta de albañil
(masonry trowel)

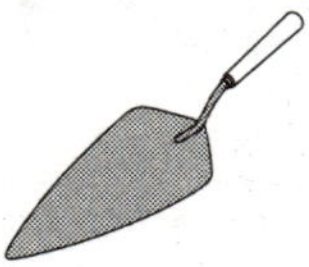

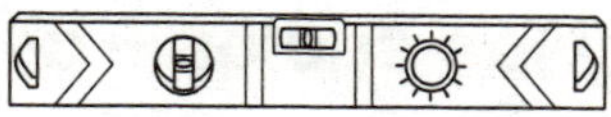

nivel de burbuja (spirit level)

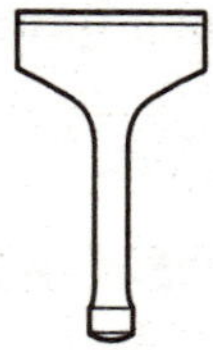

cincel de albañil
(bricklayer's chisel)

Plastering

llana de yesero
(plastering hawk)

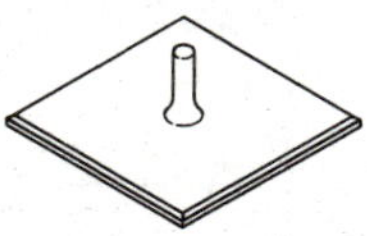

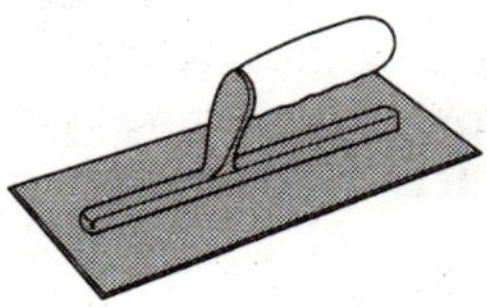

paleta de yesero
(plastering trowel)

balde (bucket)

paleta (trowel)

rascador
(shavehook)

cuchilla de enlucir
(filling knife)

balde (m)	bucket
cincel (m)	chisel
cincel de albañil	bricklayer's chisel
cubo (m)	bucket
cuchilla (f) de enlucir	filling knife
hormigonera (f)	concrete mixer

llana (f) de yesero	plastering hawk
nivel (m) de burbuja/de agua	spirit level
pala (f)	shovel
paleta (f)	trowel
paleta de albañil	masonry trowel
paleta de yesero	plastering trowel
pico (m)	pick
rascador (m)	scraper, shavehook
tamiz (m)	riddle – box with a fine mesh base for removing lumps from sand or other dry material

Los techos y los suelos – ceilings and floors

In older houses, the ceiling and floor are often – literally – two sides of the same thing! The traditional wooden floor consists of planks laid over joists, and the undersides of the planks form the ceiling. In houses without central heating, this allows the warmth from the downstairs living rooms to rise up to the bedrooms – but it also lets the noise up.

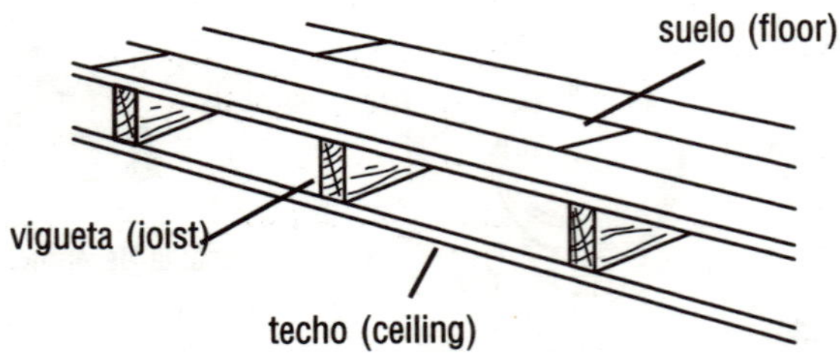

If there is a ceiling, it will be made of *un machihembrado* (thin wood panelling) or, as in the UK, of *varilla enlucida de yeso* (lathe and plaster) or *paneles de yeso* (plasterboard).

In apartments and in more modern houses, the floor may be made of reinforced concrete. Apart from better sound-proofing, this also allows the use of ceramic or stone tiles for floors in upstairs rooms. Most apartment buildings (old and new) have stone tiled floors, which cannot be laid on a flexible wood base.

machihembrado (m)	panelling (tongue and groove)
madero (m)	joist
suelo (m)	floor
techo (m)	ceiling
varilla (f) enlucida de yeso	lathe and plaster
vigueta (f)	joist

English–Spanish quick reference

The structure – la estructura

attic	desván (m)
basement	sótano (m)
balcony	balcón (m)
ceiling	techo (m)
chimney	chimenea (f)
floor	suelo (m)
foundations	cimientos (mpl)
lean-to/shed	cobertizo (m)
mould	moho (m)
party wall	pared (f) divisoria
porch	pórtico (m), porche (m)
roof	techo (m), tejado (m)
rot	podredumbre (f)
rubble	escombros (mpl)
stairs	escalera (f)
terrace	terraza (f)
wall	muro (m)
woodworm	carcoma (f)

Roofing – la techumbre

attic	desván (m)
beam	correa (f)
carpenter	carpintero de armar (m)

ceiling	techo (m)
chimney	chimenea (f)
dormer window	buhardilla ventana (f)
eaves	alero (m)
flashing	banda (f) para junta
gable	aguilón (m)
hip ridge	cresta (f) de copete
hip roof	techo (m) de cuatro aguas
lathe	varilla (f), viguetas (fpl)
oak	roble (m)
pine	pino (m)
rafter	viga (f)
ridge	caballete (m), limatesa (f)
roof	techo (m), tejado (m)
roof timbers	correas (mpl)
roof truss	armadura de techo (f)
roofer	tejador (m)
roofing felt	cartón (m) alquitranado para techumbres
skylight	tragaluz (m), claraboya (f)
slate	pizarra (f)
slate nail	clavo (m) para pizarra
sloping roof	cubierta inclinada (f)
terrace	terraza (f)
thatched roof	tejado (m) de paja
tile	teja (f)
tile, curved	teja curva/romana
valley	limahoya (f)
wood preservative	preservador (m) de madera

Walls – los muros/las paredes

air gap	cámara (f) de aire
breeze block	bloque de hormigón (celular) (m)
brick	ladrillo (m)

brick, hollow	ladrillo hueco (m)
bricklayer	albañil (m)
builder	albañil (m), obrero (m)
building (work)	albañilería (f)
cement	cemento (m)
chipboard	tablero aglomerado (m)
concrete	hormigón (m)
concrete, reinforced	hormigón armado (m)
crack (in wall)	grieta (f)
damp	humedad (f)
damp course	aislante hidrófugo (m)
excavation	excavaciones (fpl)
footing	zapata (f)
foundations	cimientos (f)
granite	granito (m)
half-timbered	de armazón de madera
insulation	aislante (m)
limestone	piedra caliza (f)
lining (for wall)	enlucido (m)
lintel	dintel (m)
marble	mármol (m)
mortar	mortero (m)
panel	panel (m), tablero (m)
partition wall	tabique (m)
plaster	yeso (m)
plaster block	bloque de yeso (m)
plasterboard	panel (m) de escayola/yeso
plasterer	enyesador (m)
quarry stone	piedra de cantera (f)
rendering	revoco (m)
rising damp	humedad (f) de paredes
rot	podredumbre (f)
rubbish	desperdicios (mpl)
rubble	escombros (mpl)

sand	arena (f)
sandstone	piedra arenisca (f)
stone	piedra (f)
stone, dressed	piedra labrada (f)
stonemason	picapedrero (m)
trench	zanja (f)
wall (external)	muro (m)
wall (internal)	pared (f)
wall tie	anclaje de muro (m)
wattle and daub	zarzo (m)

Tools – las herramientas

bucket	balde (m), cubo (m)
chisel	cincel (m)
concrete mixer	hormigonera (f)
filling knife	cuchilla de enlucir (f)
pick	pico (m)
plastering hawk	llana (f) de yesero
plastering trowel	paleta (f) de yesero
riddle	tamiz (m)
shavehook	rascador (m)
spade/shovel	pala (f)
spirit level	nivel (m) de burbuja/de agua
trowel	paleta (f)

Ceilings and floors – los techos y los suelos

ceiling	techo (m)
floor	suelo (m), solado (m)
joist	madero (m), vigueta (f)
lathe and plaster	varilla (f) enlucida de yeso
panelling	machihembrado (m)

05 la carpintería – woodwork

Almost the same...

In the UK, professionals make a distinction between carpentry, joinery and cabinet-making, though for most of us it's all woodwork. The Spanish make a similar distinction. If you want someone to work on structural timbers like floor joists or roof beams, you need *un carpintero de armar*. If you want someone to make, fit or mend fit staircases, windows, doors and the like, you need *un carpintero*. If you're looking for someone to build or restore furniture, or for decorative work, you need *un ebanista*.

One of the most obvious differences between here and Spain is in the windows. Most Spanish homes have shutters. We're fans of shutters. They keep the sun out on a summer's day, the warmth in on a winter's night, and the burglars out when you're away. A side effect of shutters is that the windows must open inwards, or slide.

There's a small but significant difference in the way they hang doors – they use split hinges. We like these too, and so will you be the next time that you are painting a door, laying floor tiles, moving big furniture or doing any other job where a door in a doorway is a nuisance. With split hinges, you just lift the door off and prop it up somewhere out of the way.

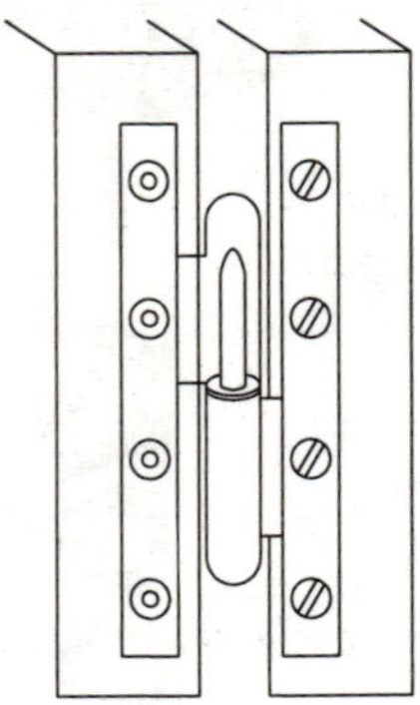

Split hinges make hanging (and unhanging) doors simple – as long as you fit them the right way up!

Check at the ayuntamiento

- Your internal fittings are entirely your affair, but if you are adding or altering external doors or windows – especially on the publicly-visible sides of the house – check with the *ayuntamiento* if the new ones are different from the others in the neighbourhood.

La carpintería interior – internal woodwork

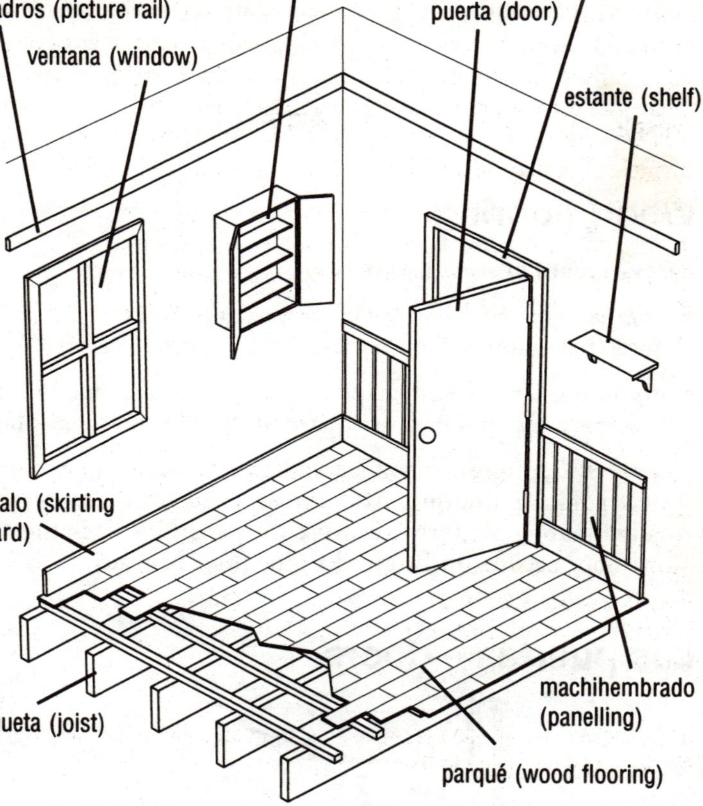

armario (m)	cupboard
armario empotrado (m)	built-in cupboard
armazón (m)	door or window frame
estante (m)	shelf
falso techo (m)	false ceiling
machihembrado (m)	panelling
marco (m)	door or window frame
moldura (f) para colgar cuadros	picture rail
parqué (m)	wood flooring

puerta (f)	door
suelo (m)	floor
tabla (f)	floorboard
tarima (f) flotante	laminate wood flooring
ventana (m)	window
vigueta (f)	joist
zócalo (m)	skirting board

Wood flooring

Parqué comes in several varieties:

- *a la inglesa* – rectangular blocks, usually laid in a brick pattern (but suitable for a herringbone pattern if preferred)
- *tipo mosaico* – small shaped wooden tiles arranged in mosaic patterns, supplied as square units on a mesh backing
- *en paneles* – pre-fab tongue-and-groove panels or wood effect laminate flooring. Also known as *tarima flotante*, literally 'floating platform', because the panels just lock together without needing to be glued to the floor beneath.

Las puertas – doors

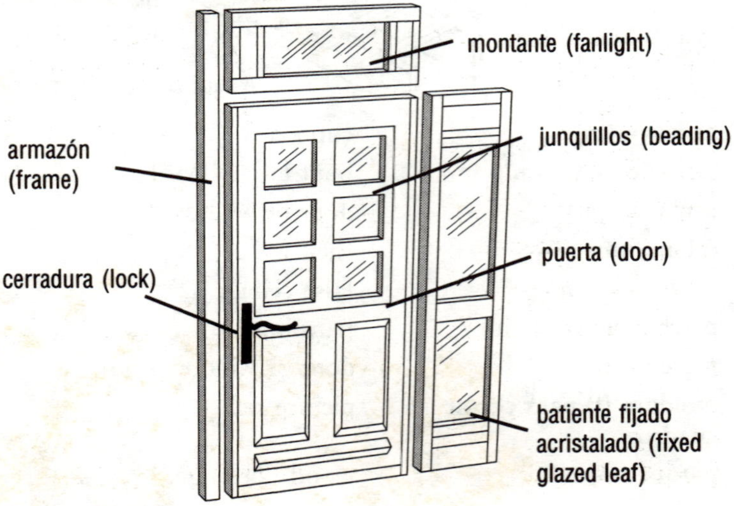

External doors may be offered as part of a complete set with matching fixed lights, glazed side panels and gap fillers.

armazón (m)	frame
arquitrabe (m)	architrave
batiente (m) fijado acristalado	fixed glazed leaf
buzón (m)	letter box
junquillos (mpl) de carpintero	wooden beading for fixing glass
manilla (f)	door handle
marco (m)	frame
masilla (f)	glazier's putty
montante (m)	fanlight
pomo (de puerta) (m)	door knob
puerta (f)	door
puerta corredera	sliding door
puerta de seguridad	high-security door
puerta deslizable	sliding door
puerta de vaivén/oscilante	swing door
tirador (m) de puerta	door handle
umbral (m)	doorstep, sill

Herrajes para puertas – hardware for doors

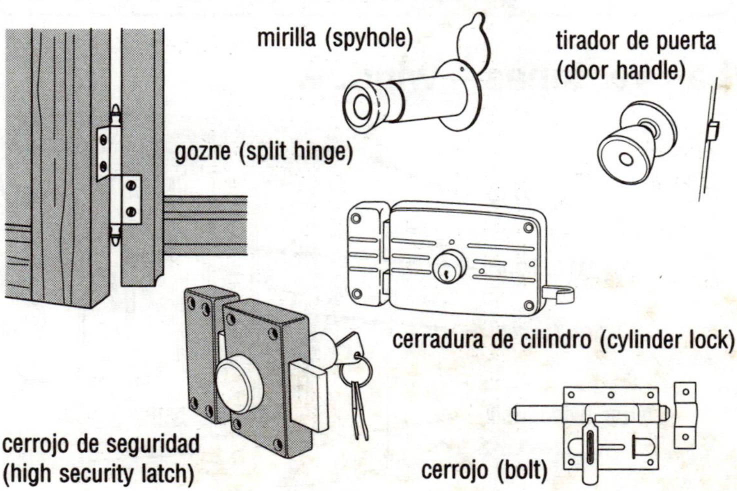

bisagra (f)	hinge
candado (m)	padlock
cerradura (f) de cilindro	cylinder lock
cerradura (f) para encastrar	mortice lock
cerrojo (m)	bolt
cerrojo de seguridad	high security latch
cerrojo para encastrar	bolt to fit into frame
cierre (m)	catch or other means of keeping a door closed
gozne (m)	split hinge
llave (f)	key
mirilla (f)	spyhole for door
ojo (m) de cerradura	keyhole
pernio de quicio (m)	strap hinge for hanging heavy doors or shutters
pestillo (m)	bolt

Watch out!

Front doors in apartment buildings generally have a *mirilla* (spyhole) to see who's outside, but they're not always the little fish-eyes you may have seen here. In older buildings, they can be large, wonderfully ornate pieces of ironwork.

Las ventanas – windows

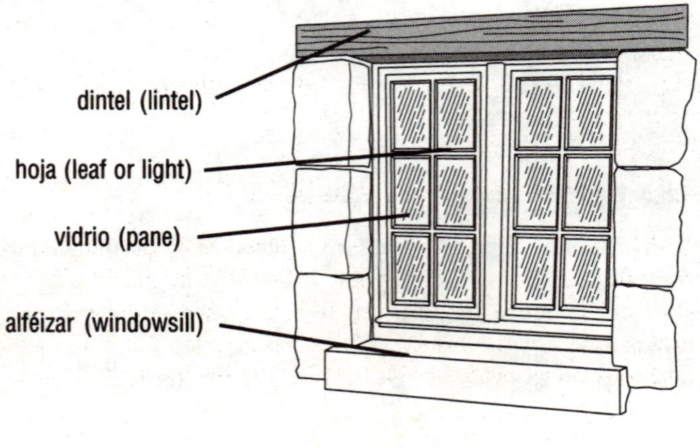

acristalamiento (m)	glazing
acristalamiento doble (m)	double glazing
alféizar (m)	windowsill
batiente (m)	leaf or light
cierre (m)	window catch
claraboya	skylight
cristal (m)	window pane
dintel (m)	lintel
hoja (m)	leaf or light
marco (m)/armazón (m)	window frame
puertaventana (f)	French window
tragaluz (m)	skylight
ventana (f)	window
ventana corredera/corrediza	sliding window
ventana de bisagras	casement window
ventana de celosía	lattice window
ventana guillotina	sash window
ventana salediza	bay window
vidrio (m)	glass
vidrio (m)	pane
vidrio doble (m)	double-glazed pane

Las contraventanas – shutters

Shutters are fitted on doors and windows to give extra security, shade and insulation. There are many styles – in wood and other materials. In this small book we only have room to cover a few of the more popular.

Las contraventanas abatibles

Conventional outward-opening shutters which open flat against the outside wall are also often called *Mallorquinas* (Majorcan-style). To secure the shutters when closed, they normally use *una falleba* or *españoleta* – a rod that holds the leaves together and locks into the top and bottom of the frame.

Contraventana (shutters) – there's a mosquito screen over the window – very useful if the house is near water.

Contraventana de machihembrado

Made from tongue and grooved wood and held together by cross pieces – *traviesas*. If there is also a diagonal brace – *un tornapuntas* – it may be known as a *Zeta* – a 'Zed'.

Contraventana persiana

Made from slats in a frame, this type derives its name from the heat of the Middle East. They provide ventilation and shade rather than insulation and shade. This kind of shutter is also known as a **Mallorquina – Majorcan-style.**

Contraventana corredera plegable

These may also be slatted, but open differently – they may fold concertina-style against the sides of the window frame, or slide away to either side of the window.

Persiana enrollable

These are made from PVC or metal, not wood, but we're going to put them here anyway! They are very common in more modern buildings. Roller shutters can be fitted inside the door or window frame, or project out from it. They can be hand-wound or electrically operated.

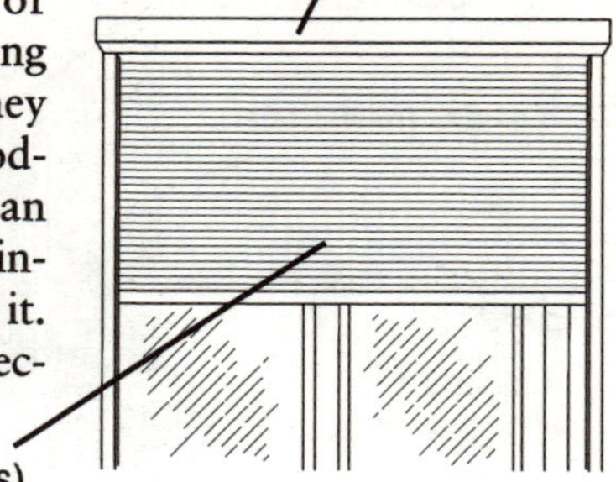

batiente (m)	leaf, single shutter
bisagra (f)	hinge
cajón para persiana enrollable	casing for roller shutter
carril (m)	tracking on roller shutters
contraventana persiana (f)	slatted shutter
cremona (f)	window/shutter lock
falleba (f)	window/shutter fastening
gozne (m)	split hinge
guía (f)	tracking on roller shutters
hoja (f)	leaf, single shutter
lamas (fpl)	shutter strips
tirante (m)	strap of hinge
pernio (m)	hinge
persiana (f)	slatted shutter
persiana corredera (f)	sliding shutter
persiana enrollable (f)	roller shutters
pestillo (m)	latch
tornapuntas (m)	diagonal brace on shutter

La escalera – staircase

barandilla (f)	rails
contrahuella (f)	riser
descansillo (m)	landing

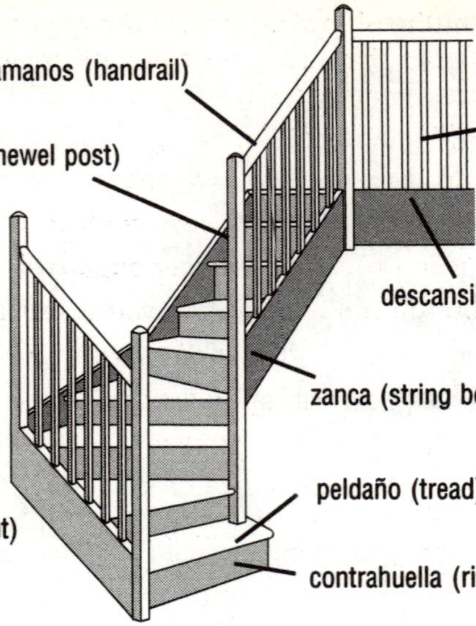

escala/escalera (f) de mano	ladder
escalera (f)	staircase
escalera de caracol	spiral staircase
escalera de tijera	step ladder
escalera plegable (de desván)	fold-away stairs (for loft)
escalerilla (f)	step ladder
pasamanos (m)	handrail
peldaño (m)	tread
pilastra (f)	pilaster, newel post
tramo (m)	flight
zanca (f)	string board

Los armarios y la estantería – cupboards and shelves

For most of us, making built-in cupboards and shelves isn't a *carpintería* job – we just head for the nearest IKEA and buy flat-packs and shelving systems. It's the same in Spain. You'll find the IKEA stores there rather few and far between, but there are local varieties such as Leroy Merlin, and in areas like the Costa del Sol, plenty of British-owned stores who are used to catering to UK tastes. Notice that the Spanish don't distinguish between storage for clothes (wardrobes) and for other uses (cupboards), they just use *armario* for everything.

armario (m)	wardrobe
armario de nicho (m)	alcove cupboard
armario de rincón (m)	corner cupboard
armario empotrado (m)	fitted wardrobe/cupboard
balda (f)	shelf (in cupboard)
barra (f) de colgar	clothes rail
cajón (m)	drawer
corbatero (m)	tie rack
costado (m)	side of cupboard
estante (m)	shelf
estantería (f)	set of shelves
llavero (m)	key hook
puertas correderas (fpl)	sliding doors
puertas plegables (fpl)	folding doors
zapatero (m)	shoe rack

La madera – wood

The wood section of a Spanish *bricolaje* (DIY store) looks much the same as one in any UK DIY store, with various shapes, sizes and varieties of woods, *cepillado* (planed) or *en bruto* (unplaned).

abeto (m)	Scandinavian pine
castaño (m)	chestnut
con ranuras y lengüetas (adj)	tongue and grooved
contrachapados (m)	plywood
contrachapados de madera noble (m)	plywood with wood veneer
DM	MDF (medium density fibreboard)
haya (f)	beech
junquillos (mpl) de carpintero	wooden beading

machihembrado (m)	tongue and grooved
madera tropical (f)	tropical hardwood
madera frondosa (f)	hardwood
madera resinosa (f)	softwood
pino (m)	pine
rechapado (m)	veneer
roble (m)	oak
tablero (m)	panel
tablero aglomerado	chipboard panel
tablero aglomerado rechapado	veneered chipboard panel
tablero de madera	wood panel
tablero duro/de fibra	hardboard panel
tablero laminado	melamine-coated panel

Las herramientas – tools

If you are going to do any *bricolaje* (also known as *hágalo usted mismo* – literally 'do it yourself'), you will need *unas herramientas* (some tools) and *una caja de herramientas* (a toolbox) – or even *un taller* (a workshop) – to keep them in. Here's an assortment of tools that you may find useful.

alicates (mpl)	pliers
barrena (f)	gimlet
berbiquí (m)	brace, of bit and brace
broca (f)	drill bit
cepillo (m)	plane
cinta métrica (m)	tape measure
clavo (m)	nail
cola para madera (f)	wood glue
cortavidrios (m)	glass cutter
cuchilla (f)	blade (e.g. for Stanley knife)
cutter (m)	cutter (Stanley knife)
destornillador (m)	screwdriver
destornillador eléctrico (m)	electric screwdriver

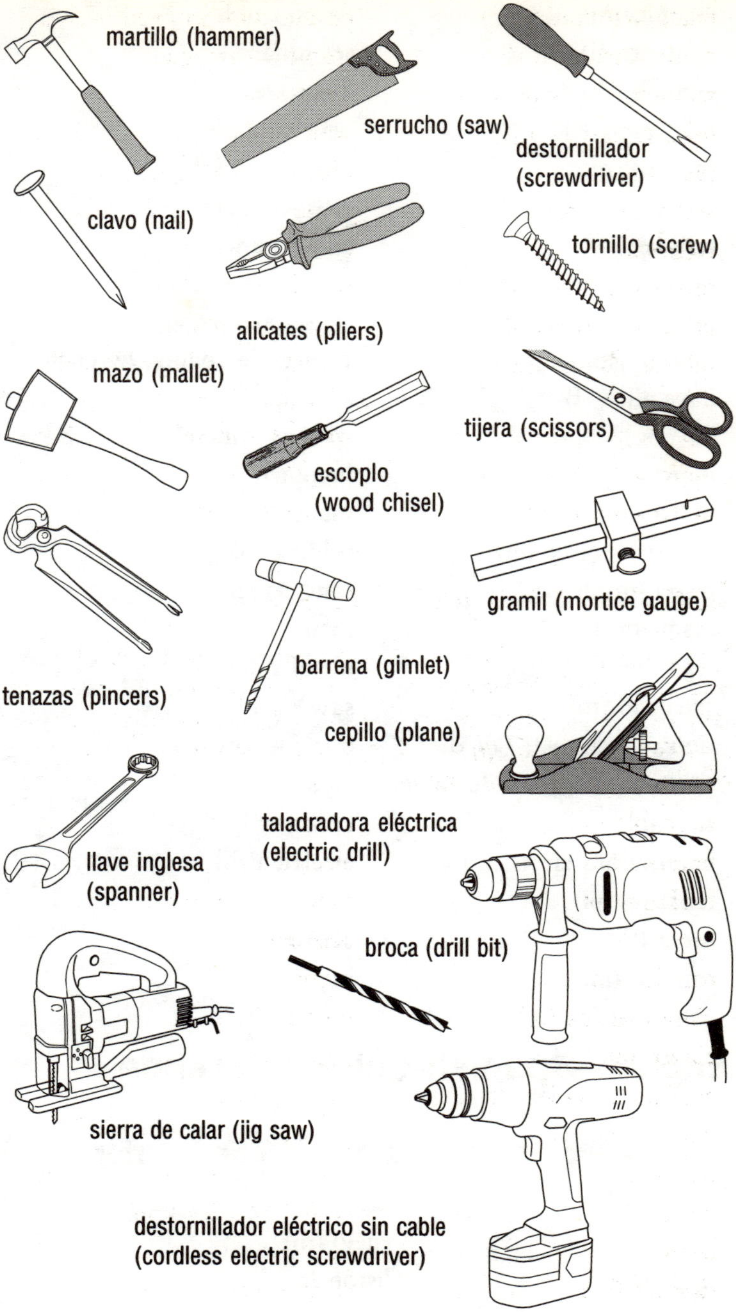
martillo (hammer)
serrucho (saw)
destornillador
(screwdriver)
clavo (nail)
tornillo (screw)
alicates (pliers)
mazo (mallet)
tijera (scissors)
escoplo
(wood chisel)
gramil (mortice gauge)
barrena (gimlet)
tenazas (pincers)
cepillo (plane)
taladradora eléctrica
(electric drill)
llave inglesa
(spanner)
broca (drill bit)
sierra de calar (jig saw)
destornillador eléctrico sin cable
(cordless electric screwdriver)

escoplo (m)	wood chisel
escuadra (f)	set square
escuadra (f) en T	T-square
falsa regla (f)	bevel square
formón (m)	mortice chisel
gramil (m)	mortice gauge
grapadora (f)	staple gun
juego (m) de llaves inglesas	set of spanners
lijadora orbital (m)	rotary sander
llave ajustable (f)	adjustable spanner/wrench
llave allen (f)	allen key
llave inglesa (f)	spanner – literally 'English key'
martillo (m)	hammer
mazo (m)	mallet
metro plegable (m)	folding rule
papel (m) de lija	sand paper
rasqueta (f)	rasp
regla metálica (f)	metal rule
serrucho (m)	saw
sierra (f) circular / de disco	circular saw
sierra (f) de calar / de vaivén	jig saw
sin cable	cordless
taladradora eléctrica (f)	electric drill
tenazas (fpl)	pincers
tijera (f)	scissors
tornillo (m)	screw

English–Spanish quick reference

Internal woodwork – la carpintería interior

cupboard	armario (m)
floor	suelo (m)
floorboard	listón (m)

frame, door or window	marco (m) or armazón (m)
joist	vigueta (f)
kitchen cupboard	alacena (f)
laminate flooring	tarima flotante (f)
panelling	machihembrado (m)
picture rail	moldura (f) para colgar cuadros
shelf	estante (m)
skirting board	zócalo (m)
wood flooring	parqué (m)

Doors – las puertas

architrave	arquitrabe (m)
beading for glass	junquillos (mpl) de carpintero
door	puerta (f)
door frame	marco (m), armazón (m)
doorstep	umbral (m)
fanlight	montante (m)
letter box	buzón (m)
sliding door	puerta corrediza/corredera (f)
swing door	puerta de vaivén (f)

Hardware for doors – herrajes para puertas

bolt	cerrojo (m), pestillo (m)
catch	cierre (m)
cylinder lock	cerradura (f) de cilindro
door handle	manilla (m)
door knob	pomo (m)
hinge	bisagra (f), pernio (m)
hinge, split	gozne (m)
key	llave (f)
keyhole	ojo (m) de cerradura
lock	cerradura (f)
mortice lock	cerradura (f) para encastrar
spyhole for door	mirilla (f)

Windows – las ventanas

bay window	ventana (f) salediza
casement window	ventana (f) de bisagras
double glazing	acristalamiento doble (m)
french window	puertaventana (f)
glass	vidrio (f)
leaf or light	batiente (m), hoja (f)
lintel	dintel (m)
pane	vidrio (m), cristal (m)
sash window	ventana (f) de guillotina
skylight	tragaluz (m), claraboya (f)
window frame	marco (m) or armazón (m)
window pane	cristal (m)
windowsill	alféizar (m)

Shutters – las contraventanas

hinge	bisagra (f)
latch	pestillo (m)
roller shutter	persiana enrollable (f)
roller shutter, casing	cajón (m) de persiana enrollable
shutter fastening	falleba (f), españoleta (f)
shutter, slatted	contraventana persiana (f)
strap hinge	pernio con tirante (m)
window/shutter lock	cremona (f)

Staircases – la escalera

flight of steps	tramo (m)
fold-away stairs	escalera (f) plegable de desván
handrail	pasamanos (m)
ladder	escalera (f), escala (f)
landing	rellano (m), descansillo (m)
newel post	pilastra (f)
rails	barandilla (f)

riser	contrahuella (f)
spiral staircase	escalera (f) de caracol
staircase	escalera (f)
step ladder	escalerilla (f)
tread	peldaño (m), escalón (m)

Cupboards and shelves – los armarios y la estantería

clothes rail	barra (f) para colgar
doors, folding	puertas plegables (fpl)
drawer	cajón (m)
fitted wardrobe	armario empotrado (m)
key hook	llavero (m)
shelf	estante (m)
shelf as part of cupboard	balda (f)
shelves, set of	estantería (f)
shoe rack	zapatero (m)
tie rack	corbatero (m)
wardrobe/cupboard	armario (f)

Wood – la madera

beech	haya (m)
chestnut	castaño (m)
chipboard	tablero (m) aglomerado
hardboard	tablero (m) duro, de fibra
hardwood	madera frondosa (f)
MDF	DM
melamine panel	tablero (m) laminado
oak	roble (m)
panelling	machihembrado (m)
pine	pino (m)
plywood	contrachapados (m)
softwood	madera resinosa (f)
tongue and grooved	con ranuras y lengüetas

veneer	rechapado (m), chapado (m)
veneered panel	tablero (m) rechapado
wood panel	tablero (m) de madera

Tools – las herramientas

allen key	llave allen (f)
bevel square	falsa regla (f)
blade	cuchilla (f)
brace, of bit and brace	berbiquí (m)
chisel	escoplo (m)
cutter (Stanley knife)	cutter (m)
drill bit	broca (f)
electric drill	taladradora eléctrica (f)
electric screwdriver	destornillador eléctrico (m)
folding rule	metro plegable (m)
gimlet	barrena (f)
glass cutter	cortavidrios (m)
hammer	martillo (m)
jig saw	sierra (f) de calar
mallet	mazo (m)
metal rule	regla metálica (f)
nail	clavo (m)
pincers	tenazas (fpl)
plane	cepillo (m)
pliers	alicates (mpl)
rasp	rasqueta (f)
sander	lijadora (f)
sandpaper	papel (m) de lija
saw	serrucho (f)
saw, circular	sierra (f) circular, de disco
scissors	tijera (f)
screw	tornillo (m)
screwdriver	destornillador (m)
set square	escuadra (f)

spanner	llave inglesa (f)
spanner, adjustable	llave ajustable (f)
spanners, set of	juego (m) de llaves
staple gun	grapadora (f)
tape measure	cinta métrica (f)
T-square	escuadra (f) en T
wood glue	cola para madera (f)

06 la fontanería – plumbing

Almost the same...

Generally plumbing systems look much the same in Spain and the UK. There are a few visible differences – bathrooms are usually fully tiled, and washbasins typically have plunger-stoppers not plugs. The important differences are not so visible.

Spanish pipe and fitting sizes are metric – as UK sizes are in theory, but Spanish sizes are properly metric while UK sizes are just conversions of the old Imperial measures. So, in the UK you have 15mm ($^5/_8$"), 19mm ($^3/_4$"), 22mm ($^7/_8$") and the like, while the Spanish sizes are 10mm, 12mm, 16mm, 20mm, etc. The upshot is that you cannot normally use British fittings in a Spanish plumbing system. Those lovely taps that you saw in your local Habitat won't fit on your bath – but don't worry, you can also find Habitat in Spain!

The second point you need to note is that Spanish houses have a direct cold water supply system – there's no cold tank. That'll give you a bit more space in the attic if you have one, but the important things in plumbing terms are that your water supply is at mains pressure, and that this is higher than you get in the UK (unless you're caught in the middle of a water shortage – see below). In the UK, mains pressure is typically 0.5 bar or less and at most 1 bar. In Spain, pressure of up to 3 bars is normal. If the pressure is too high in your area, you can fit a *reductor de presión* (regulator) to reduce it to a more reasonable level. You should definitely fit one if the pressure is above 3 bar, as many household appliances are designed with that as an upper limit.

Water supply is managed locally in Spain, either by the municipal authorities or sometimes by private companies. Connection fees vary wildly (from €60 to over €400 at the time of writing); usage is metered but there's usually a minimum amount which you pay for regardless of whether you used that much or not (*el consumo mínimo*) – effectively a standing charge.

Water shortages are not uncommon in the sunny South during dry periods, and you may find you are rationed, sometimes quite severely, unless you have a private supply. Many new community developments do have a reliable private supply, but you will pay for the privilege. One way of reducing water usage is to install taps with *aireadores*, which mix air in with the water to reduce the flow – they are much the same price as normal taps.

Check at the ayuntamiento

- If you are in a rural area and need to install *una fosa séptica* (septic tank) – also called *un pozo séptico* – you must get your plans approved at the *ayuntamiento* (see page 100).

La tubería – pipework

With modern materials and fixings, plumbing can be a job for the brave enthusiast – but even if you are not doing the plumbing yourself, it is helpful to know what the professionals are on about, and what you are paying for.

El abastecimiento – supply

The supply pipework is normally copper, though flexible braided polyethylene is increasing used to connect appliances. On copper pipes, the connections may be *soldado* (soldered) or *con rosca* (threaded, i.e. compression).

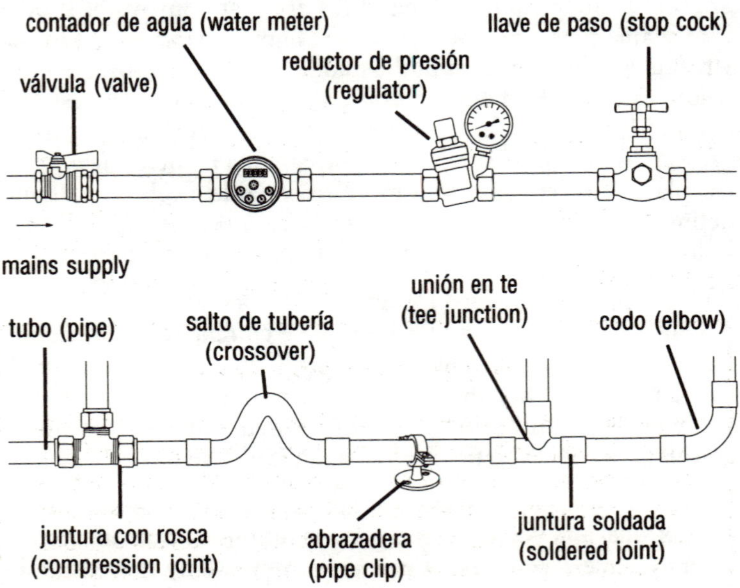

abrazadera (f)	pipe clip
agua (f) de la red de suministro	mains water

anclaje (m)	pipe clip
cobre (m)	copper
cobre recocido (m)	flexible copper, sold in rolls
codo (m)	elbow/corner joint
contador de agua (m)	water meter
grifo (m)	tap
grifo con aireador (m)	aerator tap
grifo de desagüe (m)	drain cock
juntura (f)	joint
juntura con rosca (f)	compression joint
juntura soldada (f)	soldered joint
llave (f)	tap (handle)
llave (f) de paso	stop cock
manguito (m)	sleeve
pieza (f)	joining piece
plástico (m)	plastic
plomo (m)	lead
PVC	PVC
reducción (f)	reducing joint
reductor (m) de presión	regulator – used where high pressure is a problem
salto de tubería	crossover (curved section of pipe to go over another at 90°)
tubería (f)	pipe, length of piping

The meter never lies

In some older apartment blocks there is one meter for the whole block, with the bill being shared between residents according to the size of their apartment. This may not be very economical if there are full-time residents there and you only use the flat as a holiday home, so you should look into getting your own meter fitted. You should also check your water bills carefully, and install your own meter alongside the company meter if necessary – there are reports of overcharging by some unscrupulous suppliers.

tuberías flexibles (fpl)	flexible pipes (plastic or braided polyethylene), often used to connect taps to the fixed pipes
tubo (m)	pipe
unión (f) en T	tee junction
válvula (f)	valve, sluice gate

La tubería de desagüe – waste water system

There are two systems here: *los canalones* (guttering) for *el agua de lluvia* (rain water) and the internal system for *las aguas residuales* (waste water from sinks, baths), including *las aguas fecales* (flushed from toilets).

Guttering can be installed by a roofer or a builder. Galvanised, i.e. zinc-coated, iron was commonly used for guttering, but most is now PVC. For the internal systems, carrying *las aguas residuales*, you need *un fontanero* (plumber).

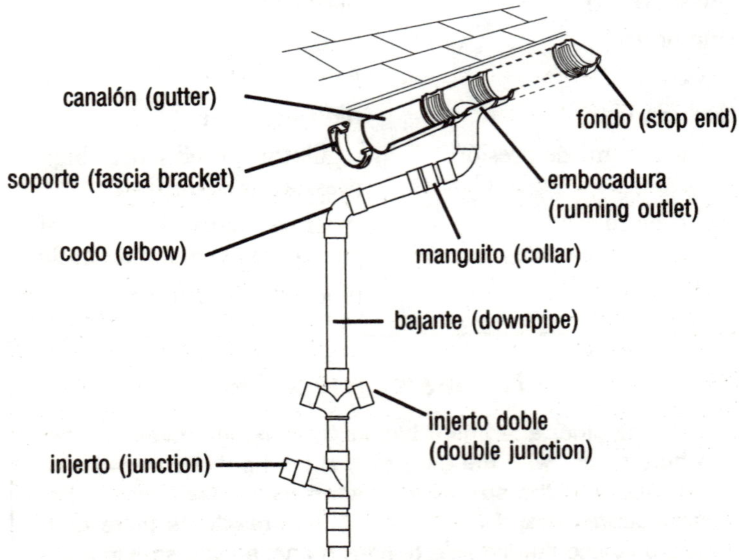

About a third of Spain is still not connected to mains sewerage – *depuradoras* (sewage treatment plants) are surprisingly rare away from major towns and cities. *Fosas sépticas* (septic tanks) are common, and dumping into cesspools or the sea still happens, but is becoming less frequent. If you are installing a waste water system, consult the *ayuntamiento* to find out whether there is a mains drain to connect to, and if not, what the other options are (see page 100).

agua (f) de lluvia	rain water
aguas (fpl) fecales	waste water from toilets
aguas (fpl) residuales	domestic waste water
bajante (m)	downpipe
canalón (m)	gutter
embocadura (f)	running outlet, joins gutter to downpipe
fondo (m)	stop end for gutter
hierro fundido (m)	cast iron
injerto (m)	junction into a downpipe
injerto doble (m)	double junction
juntura (f)	join
manguito (m)	collar, coupler
rebosadero (m)	overflow
soporte de canalón (m)	fascia bracket
tubería (f) de desagüe	waste pipes

El cuarto de baño – the bathroom

If you want a typical Spanish bathroom, you need lots of tiles – ceramic tiles on the floor and right up the walls. Tiles mean lower maintenance and easier cleaning, and cold-to-stand-on-after-a-hot-bath is not the same problem in the warmer climate. Bidets are not a universal fixture, though some Spaniards brought up on them may still find the idea of not having a bidet somehow primitive and unhygienic.

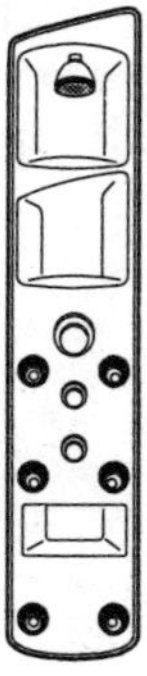

As an alternative to a shower, you can have a *hidromasaje* – one with *jets direccionales* that pound you from the side. You can buy them as *cabinas hidromasaje* (complete cubicles) or fit a *columna de hidromasaje* (hydromassage column) instead of an ordinary shower head. If you do this, make sure that your water pressure is sufficient to power it properly – and that your cubicle is watertight!

El cuarto de baño – the bathroom

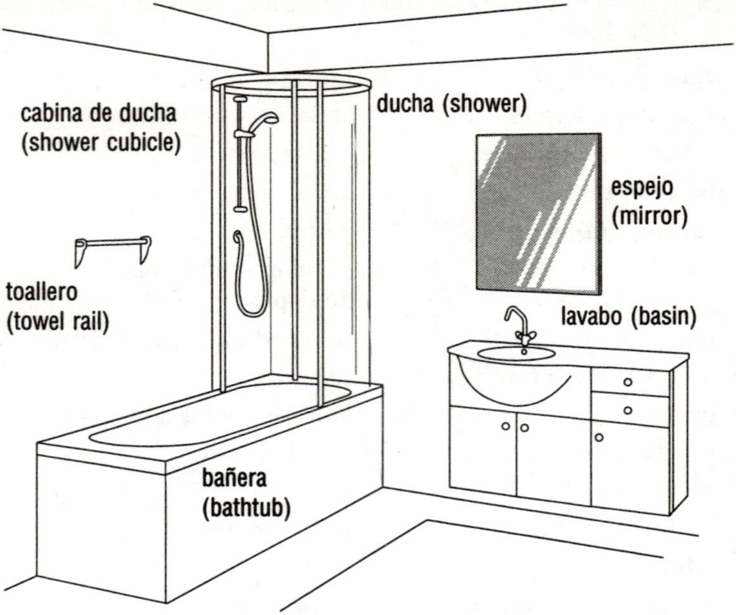

A typical modern Spanish bathroom. They often have tiled floors and walls – easy to maintain and refreshingly cool on a hot Spanish day.

El lavabo – the basin

Lever operated plughole covers are the norm for basins and baths. Mixer taps are probably more common than in the UK, and there are three main kinds: *un monobloc* (also called *un grifo de batería*) has separate hot and cold controls; *un monomando* has a single lever which controls the volume and temperature; and *un grifo extendido* has the hot and cold water controls and spout all separate (see illustration on page 99).

El lavabo – the basin

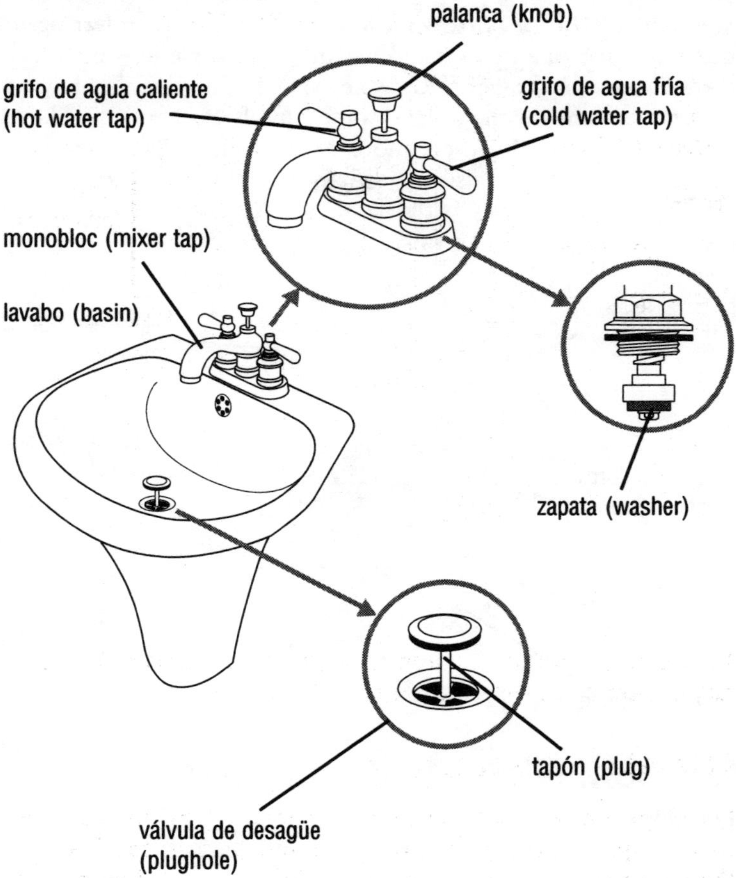

El cuenco – the washbowl

Instead of a conventional basin with taps, you could have a *lavabo* with wall mounted taps. This can be fitted *sobrepuesto* – sitting on top of a vanity unit, or *independiente* – freestanding or wall mounted.

El inodoro – the loo

We have a habit of borrowing foreign words when referring to things 'which one doesn't discuss in polite society' – our 'loo' comes from the French *l'eau* (the water). The Spanish have a variety of terms for the toilet – some equally euphemistic, like *el retrete* (the retreat), others more to the point, like *el inodoro* (the smell-less thing), also very commonly *el váter* (from 'water' closet). The technology is the same, though they seem to prefer the button flush mechanisms.

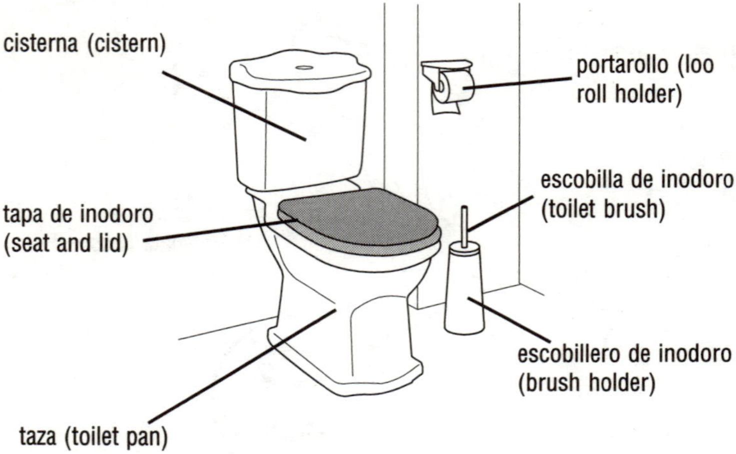

Lexicon: el cuarto de baño – the bathroom

arandela (f)	washer
armario (m) de baño	bathroom cabinet
armario (m) de medicinas	medicine cabinet
bañera (f)	bathtub
baño (m)	bathroom
báscula (f)	scales
bidé (m)	bidet
botiquín (m) de medicinas	medicine cabinet
cabina de ducha (f)	shower cubicle
calentador (m) de agua	water heater

cisterna (f)	cistern
complementos (mpl) de baño	bathroom accessories
cubo (m) de basura	rubbish bin
...con pedal (m)	pedal bin
desagüe (m)	plughole
ducha (f)	shower
escobilla (f) de inodoro	toilet brush
escobillero (m) de inodoro	toilet brush and holder
espejo (m)	mirror
estante (m) de vidrio	glass shelf
frontal (m) de ducha	shower screen
grifo (m) de agua caliente	hot water tap
grifo (m) de agua fría	cold water tap
grifo (m) extendido	mixer tap with separate controls (three-piece)
hidromasaje (m)	hydromassage cabinet/system
inodoro (m)	lavatory
jabonera (f)	soap dish
lavabo (m)	basin
llave (f)	tap handle
manopla (f)	facecloth
monobloc (m)	mixer tap with separate controls (one piece)
monomando (m)	mixer tap with combined flow/ temperature control
palanca (f)	knob/lever
palanca (f) de cisterna	flush button
papel higiénico (m)	toilet paper
plato (m) de ducha	shower tray
portarollos (m)	loo roll holder
retrete (m)	lavatory
sifón (m)	U-bend
sifón (m) de botella	bottle trap
sifón en S (m)	S-bend

suavizador (m) de agua	water softener
tapa (f) de inodoro	toilet seat/lid
tapón (m)	plug
taza (f) de inodoro	toilet pan
toallero (m)	towel rail/ring
toallero eléctrico (m)	heated towel rail
tubería (f) de desagüe	waste pipes, from basin or bath
vaciador (f)	knob/lever for plug
válvula (f) de desagüe	plughole with lever plug
zapata (f)	sealing washer (the one you change to stop a tap dripping)

La cocina – the kitchen

One of the main differences between a Spanish kitchen and its British counterpart is the oven – or lack of it. The Spanish are not great roasters or bakers, and you may find – particularly in the south – that your kitchen has a hob but no oven. Other than that, appliances and fittings are much the same.

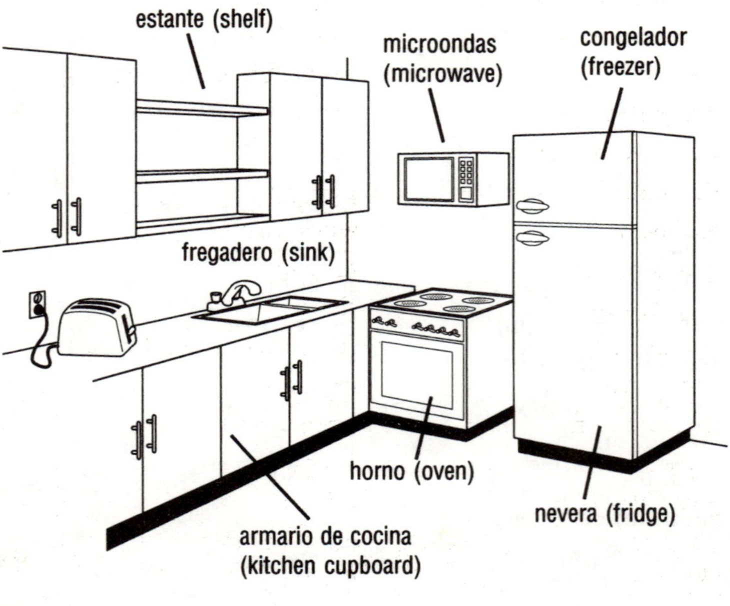

El fregadero – the sink

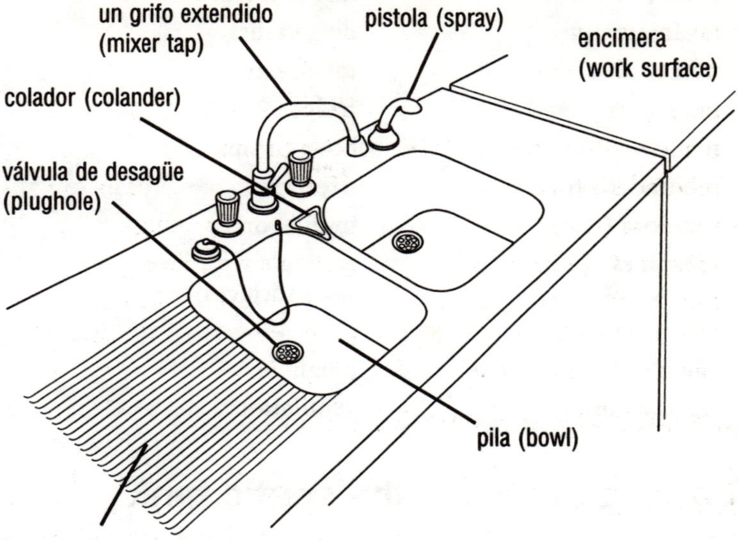

acero inoxidable (m)	stainless steel
armario de cocina (f)	kitchen cupboard
campana extractora (f)	cooker hood
cocina (f)	cooker/the act of cooking
congelador (m)	freezer
cubo (m) de basura	bin
desatascador (m)	plunger
encimera (f)	work surface
escurridor (m)	drainer
estante (m)	shelf
exterior (f)	front (doors and drawer)
fogón (m)	burner in hob
fregadero (m)	kitchen sink
frigorífico (m)	fridge
goma (f)	rubber
hornilla (f)	burner in hob
horno (m)	oven

lavadora (f)	washing machine
lavandería (f)	laundry, wash house
lavaplatos (m)	dishwasher
microondas (m)	microwave
nevera (f)	fridge
pila (f)	bowl of sink
rebosadero (m)	overflow
secadora (f)	tumble dryer
tapajuntas (m)	sealing strip (tiles/ worksurfaces)
tapón (m)	plug
válvula (f) de desagüe	plughole
ventilación (f)	ventilation

La fosa séptica – the septic tank

If your house is not connected to *el alcantarillado* (mains drains), you will need *una fosa séptica* or *un pozo séptico* (septic tank).

Are the mains coming?

Before you go any further with your plans for a new *fosa séptica*, check at the *ayuntamiento*. The Spanish are trying to put as many houses as possible onto mains drains – it's the best way to assure water quality. The aim was that all towns of 15,000 people or more would have treatment facilities by 2001, but lack of funding means this has not happened everywhere yet.

Ask at the *ayuntamiento* about the plans for your area.

But first, what is *una fosa séptica*? They vary, but essentially it is a system of chambers, dug in the ground near the house.

The first chamber is a watertight tank into which the sewer and house drains empty foul water. Solid matter is broken down by bacteriological action – a process which takes around a week. Not all solid matter breaks down, and the tank will need emptying out from time to time by a tanker, which takes the remains

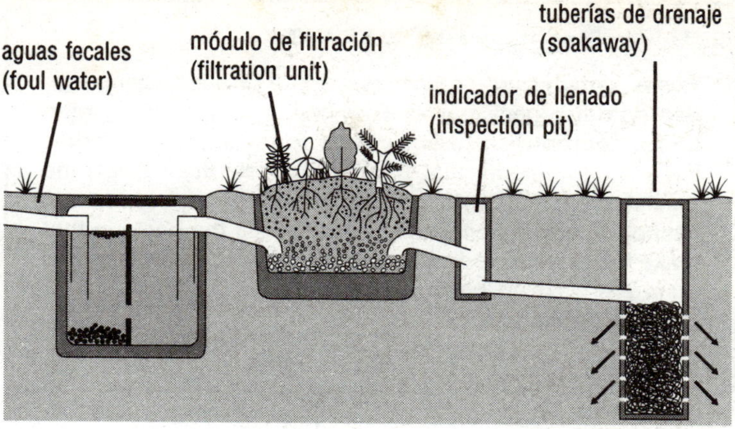

to proper treatment facilities. The length of time between visits will depend on the size of the tank and how many households are connected to it.

The second chamber is the filtration unit, typically a bed of sand. This may be closed, or capped with earth with grass or small plants growing above. (Trees and bushes must be kept away from *fosas* because their roots can damage the structures.) It may also incorporate an inspection pit to see whether the septic tank is doing its job properly or needs emptying.

The final stage is the *tuberías de drenaje* (soakaway) – pipes with holes running through a porous bed of rubble or gravel. The filtration unit and soakaway can be combined into one, or if the filtered water can be released into a stream, the soakaway may not be necessary.

The system may also have a separate grease trap, where grease, oil and other floating nasties will collect at the top, and must be removed periodically. The grease trap may be integral to the *fosa* – but the floating gunge still needs removal.

The simplest solution is probably to put the whole business in the hands of a specialist building firm. They will know the ropes, and you'll have to hire them anyway unless you want to dig those holes yourself and manhandle the tanks into place! The cost of getting them to deal with the bureaucracy will be small in comparison to the cost of the installation.

The fosa way

Fosas sépticas are organic systems that are designed for dealing with organic matter. They cannot cope with cigarette ends, tampons, *preservativos* (condoms) and other indigestible objects that people routinely flush down the toilet. Bleach, paint, white spirit, and other harsh chemicals cannot be flushed either, as these will kill the bacteria that make the system work. Ordinary soap is not a problem, and there are washing powders and cleaners that are safe for use with septic tanks.

Look after your *fosa* and your *fosa* will look after you!

aguas fecales (fpl)	foul water
indicador de llenado (m)	inspection pit
lodos (mpl)	sludge
módulo (m) de filtración	filtration unit
fosa séptica (f)	septic tank
pozo séptico (m)	septic tank
purificación (f)	purification
tuberías (fpl) de drenaje	soakaway pipes

Las herramientas – tools

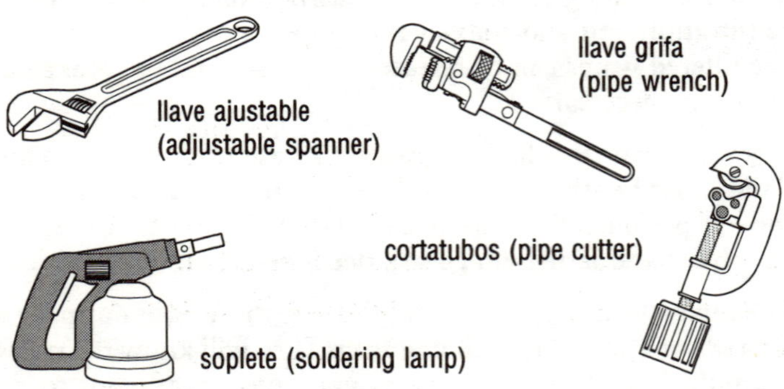

llave (inglesa) (f)	spanner
llave ajustable (f)	adjustable spanner
llave grifa (f)	pipe wrench

cortatubos (m)	pipe cutter
soplete (m)	soldering lamp
sierra (f) para metales	hacksaw
desatascador (m)	plunger

The essential plumbing term

When you need this, you won't have time to learn it, so learn it now.

¡Socorro, hay una fuga de agua! **(Help, there's a leak!)**

English–Spanish quick reference

Pipework – las tuberías

cast iron	hierro fundido (m)
copper	cobre (m)
downpipe	bajante (m)
drain cock	grifo de desagüe (m)
elbow joint	codo (m)
gutter	canalón (m)
joint	juntura (f)/pieza (f)
...compression	...con rosca
...soldered	...soldada
junction	injerto (m)/juntura (f)
lead	plomo (m)
mains water	agua(f) de la red de suministro
pipe	tubo (m), tubería (f)
pipe clip	abrazadera (f)/anclaje (m)
plastic	plástico
regulator	reductor (m) de presión
stop cock	llave (f) de paso
valve	válvula (f)

waste water system	sistema (m) de aguas residuales
water meter	contador (m)/medidor (m) de agua

Bathroom – el cuarto de baño

basin	lavabo (m), cuenco (m)
bathroom accessories	complementos (mpl) de baño
bathtub	bañera (f)
cistern	cisterna (f)
hydromassage cabinet	cabina (f) de hidromasaje
lavatory	inodoro (m), retrete (m)
medicine cabinet	armario (m) de medicinas
mirror	espejo (m)
mixer tap	monobloc (m), monomando (m), grifo extendido (m)
plug	tapón (m)
rubbish bin	cubo (m) de basura
scales	báscula (f)
shower	ducha (f)
shower cubicle	cabina (f) de ducha
soap dish	jabonera (f)
tap	grifo (m)
toilet brush	escobilla (f) de inodoro
toilet brush holder	escobillero (m)
toilet pan	taza (f) de inodoro
toilet paper	papel higiénico (m)
toilet roll holder	portarollos (m)
toilet seat lid	tapa (f) de inodoro
towel rail/ring	toallero (m)
towel rail, heated	toallero eléctrico (m)
U-bend	sifón (m)
washer	zapata (f)
waste pipes	tubería (f) de desagüe
WC seat lid	tapa (f) de inodoro

Kitchen – la cocina

basin	pila (f)
bin	cubo (m) de basura
colander	colador (m)
cooker	cocina (f)
cooker hood	campana extractora (f)
dishwasher	lavaplatos (m)
drainer	escurridor (m)
freezer	congelador (m)
fridge	nevera (f), frigorífico (m)
kitchen sink	fregadero (m)
microwave	microondas (m)
oven	horno (m)
overflow	rebosadero (m)
plug	tapón (m)
plughole	válvula (f) de desagüe
rubber	goma (f)
sink plunger	desatascador (m)
stainless steel	acero inoxidable (m)
tumble dryer	secadora (f)
washing machine	lavadora (f)
work surface	encimera (f)

Septic tank – la fosa séptica

filtration unit	módulo (m) de filtración
foul water	aguas fecales (fpl)
inspection pit	indicador (m) de llenado
purification	purificación (f)
septic tank	fosa séptica (f)/pozo séptico (m)
sludge	lodos (mpl)
soakaway pipes	tuberías (fpl) de drenaje

Tools – las herramientas

adjustable spanner	llave ajustable (f)
hacksaw	sierra (f) para metales/de arco
pipe cutter	cortatubos (m)
pipe wrench	llave grifa (f)
soldering lamp	soplete (m)
spanner	llave inglesa (f)

07 la calefacción y la electricidad – heating and electricity

Almost the same...

Heating and lighting appliances and usages are actually very similar in the UK and Spain – except of course that you're probably planning on using a lot less central heating!

With electricity, the most obvious difference is that in Spain there are several levels of power supply. Since deregulation, several firms compete in some areas, but in others there's only one supplier to choose from. In either case, electricity is relatively cheap and generally reliable, though you can expect the odd power cut in rural areas. You should install surge protection and an uninterruptible power supply if you use a computer for work.

With gas, there is a more widespread use of bottled or tank gas, because piped gas does not extend much beyond towns.

Wood is used more as a fuel outside of towns. Supplies are plentiful, prices are competitive and rural houses generally have the space to store large stocks.

La calefacción – heating

The first question is, which fuel(s) will you use?

- *leña* (firewood) is very popular – most rural Spanish houses have a wood-burning fire or *estufa* (stove). *Leños* (logs) should be stored for at least a few months before they are needed – green wood produces a lot of tar which condenses in the chimney and creates problems.
- *carbón* (coal) or *pastillas* (smokeless fuel briquettes) can be used instead of or with wood. If you want to run central heating from a solid fuel stove, coal is cheap and efficient, *pastillas* are cleaner-burning, wood is cleaner to handle.
- *fuel-oil* (oil) is widely used for central heating systems in rural areas. The installation of *un depósito de fuel-oil* (tank) is not cheap if you don't already have one, and the cost of fuel varies with the price of crude oil.
- *gas* (gas!) is supplied in three ways – piped, bottled or in a large refillable storage tank. Mains gas is often not an option in small towns and rural areas, but *bombonas de gas* (bottled butane) is cheap and widely available. You can usually

arrange for bottles to be delivered to your door, which is useful – especially if you have a top-floor flat – because they're very heavy! If you have space, you can install a large *depósito* (tank), but this is an expensive option – except in the very long term – and can push up your household insurance costs.

- *electricidad* (electricity) is cheaper in Spain than in the UK, and is worth considering as a heating fuel, especially if you use night-storage heaters (*termo-acumuladores*) to take advantage of the cheaper night-tariff electricity – although you might find that the hot water runs out quite quickly. Electric heating systems are also simpler to install than gas-fired systems.
- *energía solar* (solar power) is still surprisingly rare, given that Spain is not short of sunshine. It is well worth looking at a solar installation for heating and power needs – see page 121.

What is right for you will depend upon the nature of your house and the way that you intend to use it.

- Is there *una chimenea* (fireplace) or can one be installed?
- If the house is in an urban area, are there restrictions on solid fuel fires?
- How much storage space do you have for solid fuel, or for oil/gas tanks?
- If the house is not connected to mains gas, can it be connected, and at what cost?
- Will the house be used mainly in the summer, or at times throughout the year, or will it be your permanent home? If you only need the occasional heating on chilly evenings, the cost and efficiency of the fuel is a minor consideration.

La calefacción central – central heating

Central heating generally works by means of *radiadores*, though *calefacción del suelo* (underfloor heating) is an alternative.

A modern Spanish system is well regulated. A *sensor exterior* (external sensor) picks up the outside temperature and adjusts the temperature of the circulating water appropriately. Within the house, a *termostato de habitación* (room thermostat) will control the heat in a zone or room, while a *válvula termostática* (thermostatic regulator) can control individual radiators.

The *caldera* (boiler) can be *montado sobre la pared* (wall-mounted) or *independiente* (free-standing).

La calefacción central – central heating

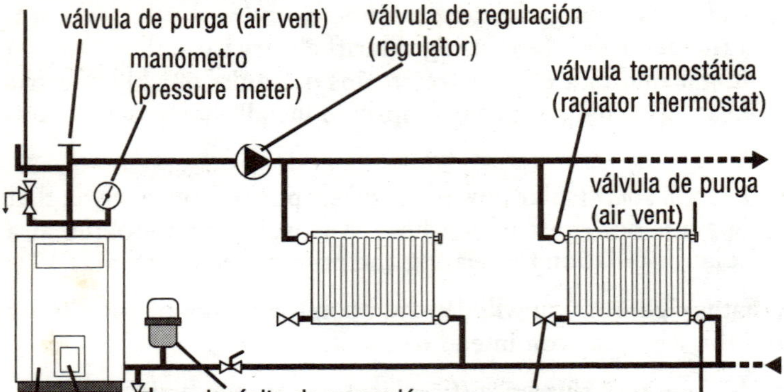

La chimenea – the fireplace

An open fire is always attractive, and as long as you don't have to do it too often (you probably won't in sunny Spain), lumping in the logs or buckets of coal and clearing out the ash can feel more like fun than a chore.

Heating and lightning

If you have a fuel-oil or propane tank it must be earthed. Some friends, enjoying a dramatic thunderstorm one night, watched in horror as lightning struck their oil tank. It glowed bright blue, but fortunately nothing else happened! They had a lightning conductor fitted the next day. Their luck didn't hold though – another strike fried their TV, video, satellite box and most of the telephone wiring in the house.

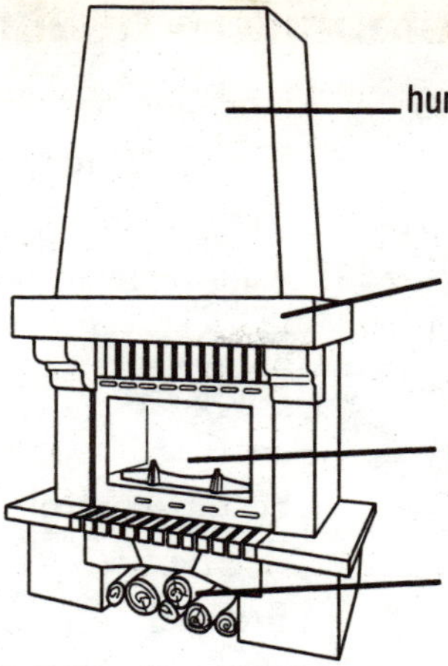

Chimeneas can be rather grand, built from thick stone and heavy beams

Los calefactores – heaters

calefactor soplador
(blow heater)

termoacumulador
(storage radiator)

emisor termoeléctrico
(radiant panel)

toallero eléctrico
(heated towel rail)

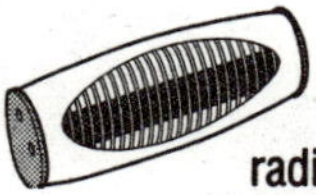

radiador infrarrojo
(infra-red heater)

chimenea eléctrica
(electric fire)

Lexicon: la calefacción – heating

alimentación de agua (f)	incoming water supply
bombona (f)	bottle, e.g. for butane
caldera independiente (f)	free-standing boiler
caldera montada a la pared (f)	wall-mounted boiler
calefactor soplador (m)	blow heater
calefactor ventilador (m)	fan heater
carbón (m)	coal
centralita de calefacción (f)	heating controls
chimenea eléctrica (f)	electric fire
contratabique (m)	fire-back
convector eléctrico (m)	convector heater
depósito (m)	tank for oil or propane
depósito (m) de expansión	expansion tank
deshollinador (m)	chimneysweep
emisor termoeléctrico (m)	radiant panel
estufa (f)	stove
estufa de gas	gas stove
estufa de leña	wood burning stove
fuel-oil	heating oil
gas LP/GLP (m)	LPG – liquid propane gas
grifo (m) de purga	drain cock
humero (m)	flue
leña (f)	firewood
leño (m)	log
llave de salida (f)	drain cock
manómetro (m)	pressure meter
quemador (m)	burner in boiler
radiador de aceite (m)	oil-filled radiator
radiador infrarrojo (m)	infra-red heater
rejilla (f) de leños	firebasket
repisa (f)	mantelpiece
sensor (m)	sensor

soplador (m)	blow heater
termoacumulador (m)	storage radiator/storage tank
termostato (m) de habitación	room thermostat
toallero eléctrico (m)	heated towel rail
válvula de purga (f)	bleeder valve, at the highest point for venting a system, or on a radiator
válvula de regulación (f)	regulator/stopcock on radiator
válvula de seguridad (f)	safety valve
válvula termostática (f)	radiator thermostat

El suministro de electricidad – the electricity supply

If you are having your electrical supply installed or reinstalled, you will have to decide which *intensidad* (power supply level) will best suit. There are several possible power ratings, ranging upwards from about 3kW. This would probably suffice for a holiday home with low power needs, but you'll need more like 9kW if you're going to spend more time there. If you're planning on electric heating, you'll want at least 12kW.

- 6kW will be enough to power simultaneously the lights, three or four small appliances, e.g. TV, fridge, vacuum-cleaner, and a single larger appliance such as a washing machine.
- 9kW will also handle a second large appliance.
- 12kW is the minimum if electricity is also used for heating, and would be sufficient for a house of up to 100m^2.
- 15kW will handle the power and heating for a larger house.

Power down

Power cuts are not uncommon, especially in rural areas, and are mainly caused by damage to the overhead power lines. If you intend living in Spain all year round, you should think about installing a back-up generator. Ask the locals how much of a problem power cuts are in your area.

The incoming electricity supply, up to the *contador* (meter) and the *interruptor general* (mains switch), is the responsibility of the supply company.

Los fusibles y los interruptores – fuses and circuit breakers

A modern *cuadro de reparto* (distribution board) doesn't have *fusibles* (fuses), but instead has an *interruptor* or *corta-circuitos* (circuit breaker) on each branch.

The best *interruptores* are the differential variety, which give greater protection against electric shocks. They have a normal magno-thermal cut-out which is triggered by a surge in the voltage or a short circuit, and a cut-out which is triggered if there is an earth fault anywhere in the circuit (e.g. from a faulty shaver to the bathroom floor, via you and your wet feet).

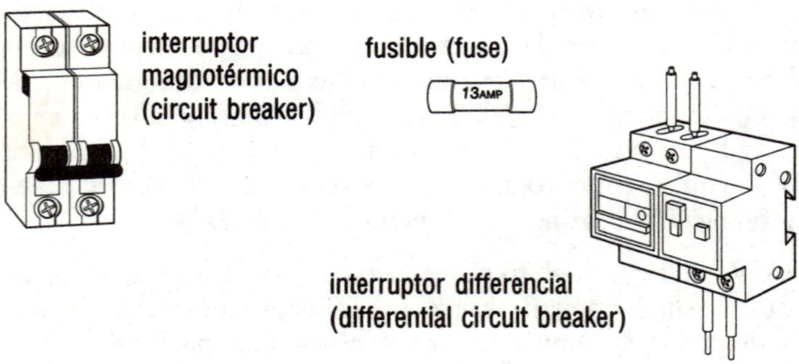

Sockets

Modern Spanish *tomas de corriente* (electric sockets) have two round holes for the *fase* (live) and *neutro* (neutral) pins, plus two flat earth contacts. Older sockets may just have live and neutral holes, and older plugs will match. Most new appliances have matching contacts for the socket's earth contacts, though some – lamps, for instance, and also appliances designed to fit shaver sockets – will just have the two pins.

UK 230 volt appliances will work perfectly well on Spanish 220 volt supply – as long as you have plug adaptors – but it's usually best to buy Spanish. You don't have the plug problem and it's easier to take it back if it doesn't work. If your house has a 110 volt supply, you will need transformers.

Note the same word, *enchufe*, is used for both 'plug' and 'socket'. If you need to be specific, ask for *una clavija* or *un enchufe macho* for a plug or *una toma de corriente* or *un enchufe hembra* for a socket.

Telephone connectors are also different to those in the UK, so make sure you get an adapter or have the cable re-crimped with an RJ11 connector – or buy your phones in Spain as well.

La electricidad – electricity

adaptador de 2/3/4 tomas	multi-socket (2/3/4 sockets)
alimentación de electricidad (f)	electrical supply
cable (m)	cable
contador (m)	meter
cordón (m)	cord, lead
corriente alterna (f)	AC
corriente continua (f)	DC
corriente eléctrica (f)	electric current
corta-circuitos (m)	circuit breaker
cortocircuito (m)	short circuit
cuadro de reparto (m)	distribution board
enchufe (m)	plug or socket
fase (f)	live wire
funda (f) de cordón	cable cover
fundir los fusibles	blow the fuses
fusible (m)	fuse
fusible de cartucho	cartridge fuse
hilo (m)	wire
hilo fusible (m)	wire fuse
intensidad (f)	power level
interruptor differencial (m)	differential cut-out
interruptor general (m)	mains supply switch
interruptor magnotérmico (m)	circuit breaker
medidor (m)	meter
neutro (m)	neutral wire

PIA (Pequeño Interruptor Automático) (m)	circuit breaker
tensión (f)	voltage
tierra (f)	earth
toma 2P + T	plug with earth plates – 2 Polos (poles) + Tierra (earth)
voltaje (m)	voltage

Short/break!

Watch out for the very similar terms *cortocircuito* and *cortacircuitos*. *Cortocircuito* (short circuit) comes from *corto* (short) – think of the 'o' in *corto* and short. *Cortacircuitos* (circuit breaker) comes from *cortar* (to cut) – remember the 'a' in *corta* and break.

Los calentadores de agua – water heaters

There are two main types of *calentador* – on-demand boilers, either gas or electric, which are all but identical to those in the UK, and the electric *termo-acumuladores* (hot-water storage heaters), which are somewhat different.

These slim cylinders are wall-mounted or free-standing, depending on size, and almost always in white enamel. The power of the heating element varies, but most are designed to slowly heat a full tank overnight, using cheap-rate electricity. They are also available with a rapid heating option, but check what *intensidad* your electricity is supplied at – the rapid heaters have a 12kW heating element.

termo-acumulador (electric water storage heater)

Los electrodomésticos – electrical appliances

The electrical appliances are broadly the same in Spain and the UK – hardly surprising as they are mostly from the same firms.

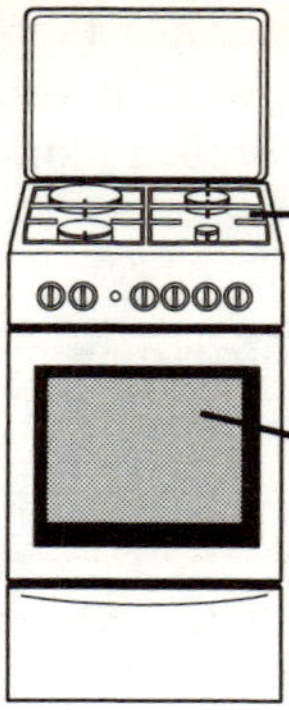

cocina (cooker)

lavaplatos (dishwasher)

lavadora (washing machine)

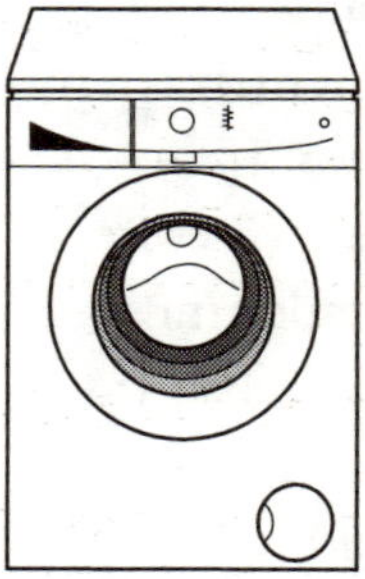

armario bodega (wine store)

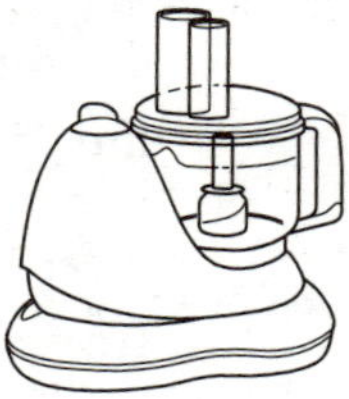

robot (food processor)

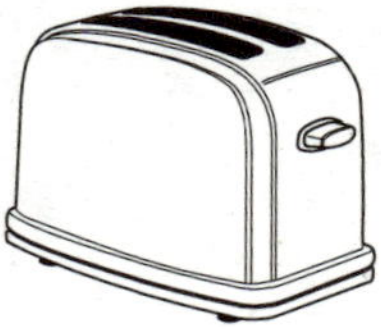

tostador (toaster)

televisor (TV)

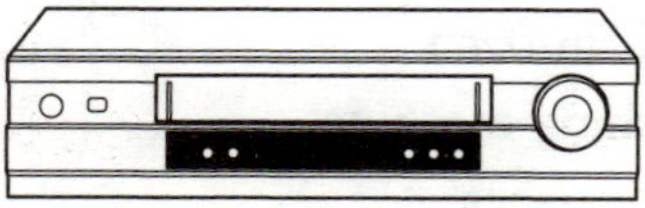

vídeo (video recorder/player)

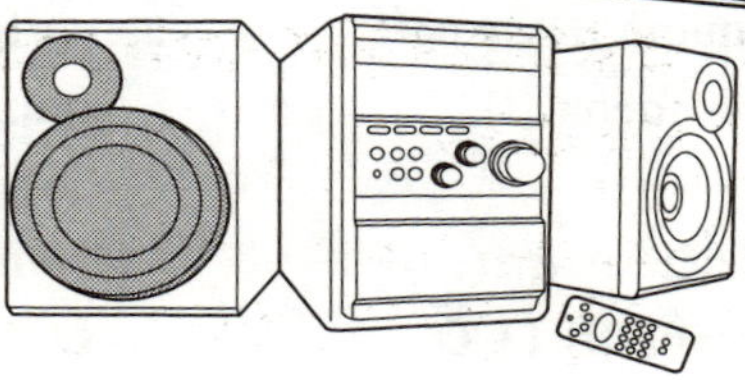

minicadena (hi-fi mini-stack)

You may have to hunt around a little to find *un hervidor* (kettle), as they are not regularly used by the Spanish. Well, if you don't drink tea and you have a *cafetera* and a *sacacorchos* (cork screw), what's the point of a kettle?

Los electrodomésticos – electrical appliances

altavoz (m)	speaker
amplificador (m)	amplifier
armario (m) bodega	(electric) wine cabinet, controlled temperature and humidity
aspirador (m)	vacuum cleaner
batidora (f)	food mixer
cafetera (f)	coffee maker (stove top)
cafetera (f) espresso	espresso machine
calentador (m) de agua	water heater
cámara (f) de video	video camera
cocina (f)	cooker
combi (m)	integrated audio-visual appliance – e.g. TV with built-in video, or video and DVD player
congelador (m)	freezer
contestador automático (m)	answering machine
digital	digital
fogón (m)	burner
funda (f) de cordón	cable cover
hervidor (m)	kettle
hornilla (f)	hob
horno (m) de encastrar	built-in oven
lavadora (f)	washing machine
lavaplatos (m)	dishwasher
máquina (f) de café	coffee machine
minicadena (f)	mini hi-fi stack system
nevera (f)	fridge
ordenador (m)	computer, PC
pantalla (f) LCD	LCD screen

pantalla plana (f)	flat screen
pantalla panorámica (f)	widescreen
pantalla plasma (f)	plasma screen
plancha (f)	iron
radio (f)	radio
radiocasete (m)	radio cassette player
reproductor casete (m)	tape deck
reproductor CD (m)	CD player
reproductor DVD (m)	DVD player
robot (m) de cocina	food processor
secadora (f)	tumble dryer
sintonizador (m)	radio tuner
teléfono (m)	telephone
televisor (m)	TV
termo-acumulador (m)	hot water storage heater
tostador (m)	toaster
vídeo (m)	video recorder/player

La iluminación – lighting

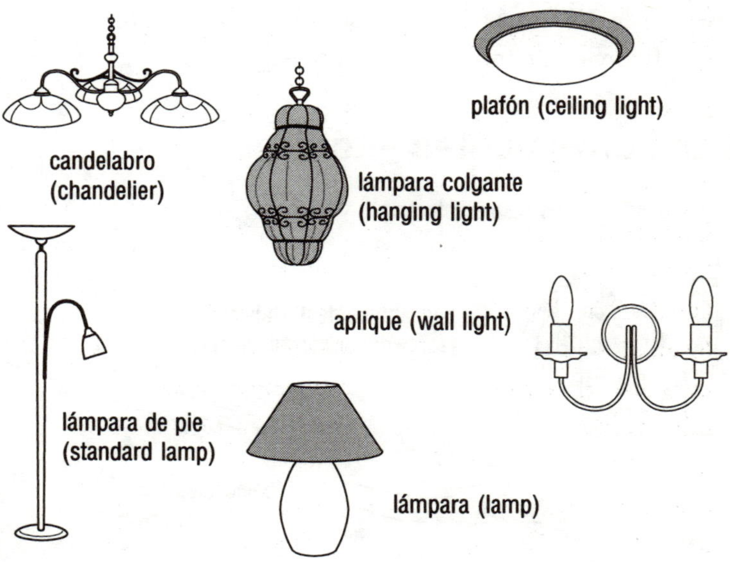

aplique (m)	wall light
araña(f) de luces	multi-bulb centre light, chandelier – literally a ‘light spider’
bombilla (f)	light bulb
candelabro (m)	chandelier
flexo (m)	reading lamp
foco (m)	spotlight
halógeno (m)	halogen
iluminación (f)	lighting
interruptor (m)	light switch
lámpara (f)	lamp
lámpara colgante	hanging light
lámpara de cabecera	bedside light
lámpara de pie	standard lamp
lámpara de estudio	reading lamp
luz (f)	light (as in the rays of light, not the thing which emits them!)
pantalla (f)	lamp shade
plafón (m)	ceiling light
portalámparas (m)	light socket
regleta de 3/4 focos (f)	strip with 3/4 spot lights
tubo fluorescente (m)	fluorescent light

Las herramientas – tools

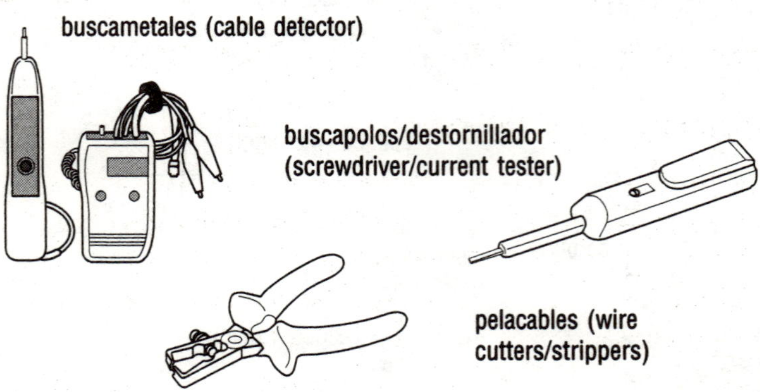

There are few special tools for electrical work – although they make electrician's versions of hammers, screwdrivers, knives and other tools.

buscametales (m)	cable detector
cinta aislante (f)	insulating tape
buscapolos (m)	current tester
...tipo destornillador	... (screwdriver)
multímetro (m)	multimeter
pelacables (m)	wire cutters/strippers

La energía solar – solar energy

It is a common myth that you need a lot of sun for solar energy. There are two kinds of solar installation – direct water heating systems (which do need lots of sunshine), and photovoltaic cells for generating electricity (which don't). Even in the UK an average household can generate around 75% of its electrical energy needs from a rooftop installation. So in Spain, you should be more than fine (even if you do live on the plain, where we are told the rain mainly falls...).

Termo-acumuladores solares (direct water heating systems) are not too expensive to install and are likely to suffice for the needs of a holiday home. For long-term residents, it's worth considering *fotovoltaicos* – although the cost of installation is higher, it will save you money in the long term. Renewable energy is also being promoted by national and international authorities keen to address climate change, so there may be EU or government grants available.

English–Spanish quick reference

Heating – la calefacción

bleeder valve	válvula de purga (f)
blow heater	calefactor soplador (m)
boiler	caldera (f)
central heating controls	centralita (de calefacción) (f)
chimneysweep	deshollinador (m)
cinder tray	cenicero (m)

coal	carbón (m)
convector heater	convector eléctrico (m)
electric fire	chimenea eléctrica (f)
firebasket	rejilla (f) de leños
firewood	leña (f)
flue	humero (m)
heated towel rail	toallero eléctrico (m)
heating oil	fuel-oil
infra-red heater	radiador infrarrojo (m)
mantelpiece	repisa (f)
radiator	radiador (m)
radiator thermostat	válvula (f) termostática
sensor	sensor (f)
storage radiator	termo-acumulador (m)
stove	estufa (f)

Electricity – la electricidad

AC	corriente alterna
cable cover	funda (f) de cordón
circuit breaker	interruptor (m), cortacircuitos (m)
distribution board	cuadro de reparto (m)
earth (wire)	tierra (f)
electric current	corriente eléctrica (f)
electrical supply	alimentación (f) de electricidad
fuse	fusible (m)
fuse wire	hilo fusible (m)
fuse, cartridge	fusible (m) de cartucho
live wire	fase (f)
mains switch	interruptor (m) general
meter	contador (m)/medidor (m)
neutral wire	neutro (m)
plug/socket	enchufe (m)
power level	intensidad (f)
short circuit	cortocircuito (m)

socket	toma (f)
voltage	tensión (f)

Electrical appliances – los electrodomésticos

amplifier	amplificador (m)
answering machine	contestador automático (m)
CD player	reproductor CD (m)
coffee machine	máquina (f) de café
computer	ordenador (m)
cooker	cocina (f)
dishwasher	lavaplatos (m)
DVD player	reproductor DVD (m)
espresso machine	cafetera (f) espresso
food mixer	batidora (f)
food processor	robot (m) de cocina
freezer	congelador (m)
fridge	nevera (f), frigorífico (m)
hob	fogón (m)
iron	plancha (f)
kettle	hervidor (m)
mini hi-fi stack system	minicadena (f)
oven	horno (m)
radio	radio (f)
radio cassette player	radiocasete (m)
radio tuner	sintonizador (m)
tape deck	reproductor casete (m)
telephone	teléfono (m)
toaster	tostador (m)
tumble dryer	secadora (f)
TV	televisor (m)
vacuum cleaner	aspiradora (f)
video camera	cámara (f) de vídeo
video recorder/player	vídeo (m)
washing machine	lavadora (f)

widescreen	pantalla panorámica (f)
wine cabinet	armario (m) bodega

Lighting – la iluminación

bedside light	lámpara (f) de cabecera
bulb	bombilla (f)
ceiling light	plafón (m)
chandelier	araña (f) de luces/candelabro (m)
fluorescent light	tubo fluorescente (m)
hanging light	lámpara colgante (f)
lamp	lámpara (f)
light	luz (f)
light fitting	portalámparas (m)
light switch	interruptor (m)
reading lamp	lámpara (f) de estudio, flexo (m)
spotlight	foco (m)
wall light	aplique (m)

08 la decoración – decorating

Almost the same...

Spanish style in decoration and furnishings is not enormously different to ours. Obviously, you will find a huge variety and range of styles in people's houses in Spain, just as you will in the UK, and these ranges very largely overlap. You will find plenty of modern-styled houses and apartments whose interiors are virtually indistinguishable from their UK counterparts (they have IKEA there too). But, just as the Spanish are never afraid to use 14 words where one will do, their furniture and furnishings tend to go that extra mile in terms of ornate patterns, intricate mouldings or gold braiding. 'Understated' is not a term you immediately associate with the Iberian outlook on life!

Some things are different for practical reasons. We have carpets in the UK to keep our feet warm and stop draughts whistling up through the floorboards. When it's 35°C outside you want a nice stone tiled floor to cool your roasting toes on. The change in climate, in vista, in the pace of life may all contribute to you adopting some elements of local style – but in the end, it's your house, and it should look the way you want it to.

Check at the ayuntamiento

- If you are thinking about painting the outside walls or the shutters, look around at your neighbours' houses first. If they all use the same colours, or a very restricted range of colours, the area may have rules on external decorations. Ask at the *ayuntamiento* before you paint anything. It will only take 10 minutes and it could save you days of repainting.
- Likewise, if you live within sight of a historic building, check at the *ayuntamiento* before you paint the outside.

La pintura – paint

Spanish paint is much the same as in the UK – you get the same types in the same sized tins (no surprise there, it's mostly made by the same companies!). The colour range may be a little unfamiliar, but let's face it – you can't really go by the names of colours in English anyway. What colour *is* 'summer orchard haze', exactly? Or 'millpond mist' or 'berry glow'? The only sure way to get the paint you want is to make liberal use of colour cards and tester pots, just as it is over here.

If a paint is *al aceite*, it is oil-based. Other types of paints are *acrílica* (acrylic), *vinílica* (vinyl), *poliuretano* (polyurethane), *microporoso* (micro-porous for external woodwork), *al esmalte* (enamel) for metalwork and special paints such for *piscinas* (swimming pools) and *fachadas* (exterior walls).

El acabado (the finish) can be *mate* (matt), *satinado* (satin), *sedoso (*silk) or *brillante* (gloss).

If you want a non-drip paint, ask for *anti-goteo*, and for one-coat paint, ask for *monocapa*. (And good luck to you – one coat never does it for us!)

acabado (m)	finish, e.g. matt/satin
acrílica	acrylic
aerosol (m)	aerosol
aguarrás (m)	white spirit
anti-goteo	non-drip
barniz (m)	varnish
bote (m) de prueba	test pot
brillante	gloss
emulsión (f)	emulsion
mate	matt
microporoso	microporous
monocapa	one-coat
pintura (f)	paint
pintura al aceite	oil-based paint
pintura de imprimación	primer
pintura para fachadas	exterior wall paint
satinado	satin finish
sedoso	silk
subcapa (f)	undercoat
tinte (m) para madera	wood stain
trementina (f)	turpentine

Las herramientas – tools

andamio (m)	scaffold
brocha (f)	large flat brush
caballete (m)	trestle
cinta (f) de enmascarar	masking tape
cubeta (f) de pintura	paint tray
manga (f) de rodillo	roller sleeve
pincel (m)	small brush (mostly round)
mango telescópico (m)	telescopic handle (for roller)
rodillo (anti-gota) (m)	roller
sábana (f)	dust sheet
tabla (f)	board to make a trestle table
trapo (m)	rag

Round brushes

Round paint brushes are more popular in Spain than they are in the UK. You have to adjust your technique a little, but you can get a good edge with them.

Los revestimientos de paredes – wall coverings

If you don't fancy painted walls, you could go for *papel pintado* (wallpaper) or *un revestimiento textil* (textile wall covering). These have the advantage of covering up minor imperfections without all the filling and smoothing you'd have to do before painting. There is also *tejido de vidrio* (glass fibre wall covering), a tough alternative to lining paper that can give a smooth finish to cracked walls and ceilings (only minor cracks – it won't hold rotting plaster together). Glass fibre for walls is more commonly found as an adhesive tape – stick it over a crack to help prevent it re-opening, then smooth and paint as normal.

cola (f)	paste
cola para papel pintado	wallpaper paste
papel para forrar (m)	lining paper

papel pintado (m)	wallpaper
papel preencolado (m)	ready-pasted wallpaper
papel vinílico (m)	vinyl wallpaper
placa (f) de corcho	cork tile
revestimiento (m) de paredes	wall covering
tejido de vidrio (m)	glass fibre wall covering

Los revestimientos textiles – wall textiles

Instead of wallpaper, you could decorate your walls with some kind of *tejido* (textile). If these are natural fibres, e.g. cotton or silk, the sheets must be fitted onto battens, with a polystyerene or other thick liner. Synthetics can also be hung this way, but can also by pasted directly onto the wall.

algodón (m)	cotton
arpillera (f)	hessian
fieltro (m)	felt
franela (f)	flannel
lana (f)	wool
seda (f)	silk
tejido (m)	fabric
terciopelo (m)	velvet

Las herramientas – tools

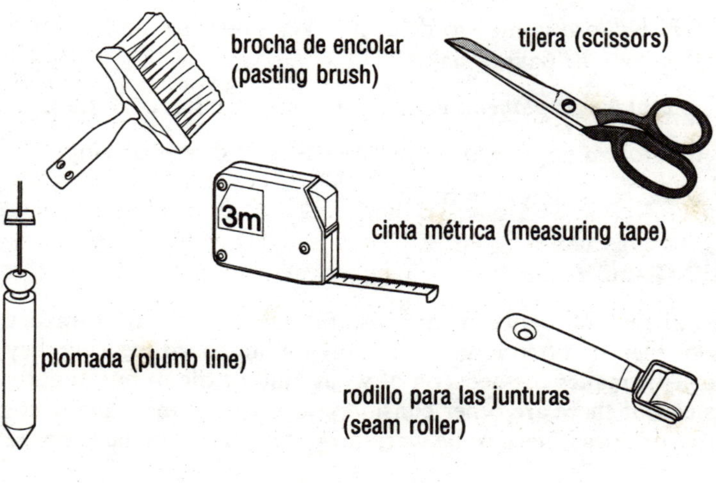

alisador (m)	wallpaper smoother
brocha (f) de encolar	pasting brush
brocha de empapelador (f)	wallpaper brush
cinta métrica (m)	measuring tape
cordel (m)	string
cortador universal (m)	Stanley knife
cutter (m)	Stanley knife
espátula (f)	filling knife
esponja (f)	sponge
máquina (f) de vapor	steam paper stripper
mesa (f) de encolar	pasting table
nivel (m) de burbuja/de agua	spirit level
plomada (f)	plumb line
raspador de papel pintado (m)	paper stripper
rodillo (m) para las junturas	seam roller
tijera (f)	scissors

El alicatado – tiling

There are several Spanish words that translate to tile, but they refer to different situations and materials:

- *un azulejo* is the word when you mean a wall tile (usually ceramic, but could be some other kind, e.g. mirrored glass).
- *una baldosa* is the word for a heavy floor tile, and also for flagstone or paving slab.
- *una placa* or *plancha* is the word for large flat cork tiles.
- *una loseta* applies to larger sheet tiles of carpet or vinyl.
- *mosaico* is simply 'mosaic'.

Tile quality

The distinction between *azulejos* and *baldosas* is partly on size (floor tiles are often larger) but more on how hard-wearing they are. This makes the decision of what kind of tile to buy slightly easier, but there are other considerations too: is the tiling decorative or does it need to be waterproof? Is it likely to be exposed to harsh chemicals or frost? Check the packaging for references to its *uso* (usage) – *interior/exterior*, *cuarto de baño* (bathrooms), *duro* (hard), *alta resistencia* (highly resistant).

In case you are interested, tiles are classified according to a schema drawn up by the standards body *Asociación Española de Normalización y Certificación* (AENOR), which rates them on their resistance to water, scratches, impact, heat, frost, chemicals, etc. It's very detailed and will enable you to make the perfect tile choice – if you have lots of time on your hands and a good head for figures!

alicatado (m) de pared	wall tiling
azulejo (m)	tile
azulejo cerámico (m)	ceramic tile
azulejo espejado (m)	mirror tile
baldosa (f)	floor tile
cemento cola (m)	tile cement
cortador (m) de baldosas	tile cutter
espátula dentada (f)	glue spreader
placa (f) de corcho	cork tile
tenazas (fpl) de alicatador	tile pincers

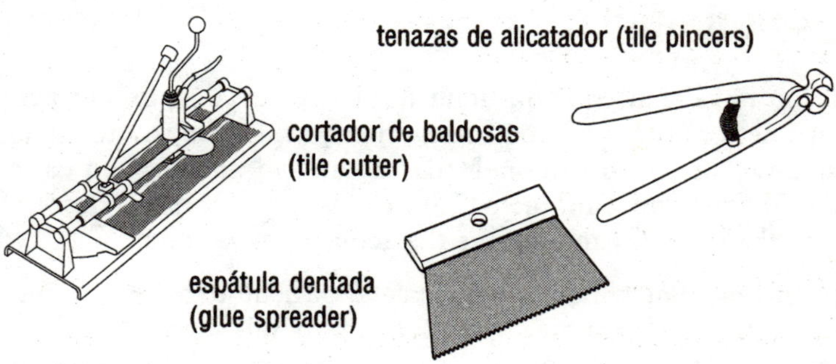

Los revestimientos de suelos – floor coverings

The Spanish simply do not use carpets and vinyls as much as we do, so don't expect to find the same choices or the same prices. They have gone for wood laminates in a big way, as we have in the UK, so there's plenty of those. But the traditional Spanish house has tiled floors in the kitchen, bathroom, conservatory and similar hard-worn places, and a lot of solid parquet elsewhere. Learn from the locals. They have been living with their climate all their lives. Bare tiled and wood floors are cooler in the summer and easy to keep clean all year round.

alfombra (f)	rug
linóleo (m)	lino
moqueta (f)	carpet
parqué (m)	wood flooring (solid or laminates)
parqué a la inglesa	rectangular blocks of solid wood
parqué en paneles	tongue-and-groove panels or wood-effect laminate flooring
parqué mosaico	small wooden tiles arranged in mosaic patterns, supplied as squares on a mesh backing
tarima flotante (f)	wood laminate flooring
vinilo (m)	vinyl flooring

Las cortinas y los estores – curtains and blinds

If you have shutters, you don't need any curtains, except perhaps net ones to give you some privacy when the shutters and windows are open – though that doesn't mean that you can't have them if you want them. They can be a key part of a decorative scheme, and can improve the acoustics of a room.

Inward-opening windows may make it difficult to hang curtains, but they make it almost impossible to fit blinds across the whole aperture. The simple solution is to fit slim blinds called *fraileros* directly to the windows.

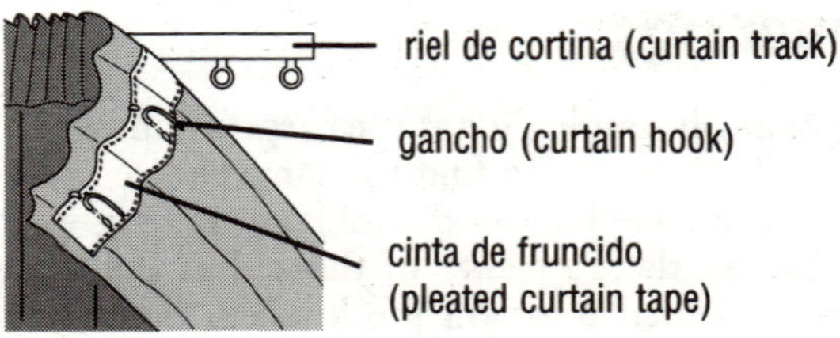

barra de cortina (f)	curtain rod
cinta (f) de fruncido	curtain tape
estor (m)	blind
frailero (m)	slim blind fitted to windows
galería (f)	curtain pelmet
persiana (f)	blind
riel (m) de cortina	curtain track
gancho (m)	curtain hook
topes rodillos (mpl)	curtain runners
tul (m)	netting
veneciana (f)	venetian blind
visillo (m)	net curtains

Los muebles – furniture

La sala de estar y el comedor – the living room and the dining room

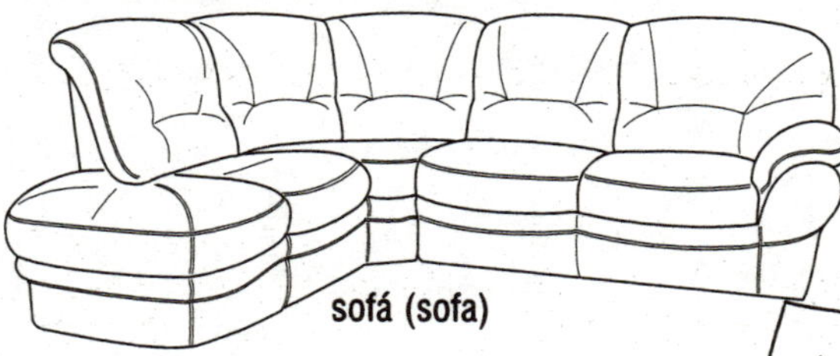

sofá (sofa)

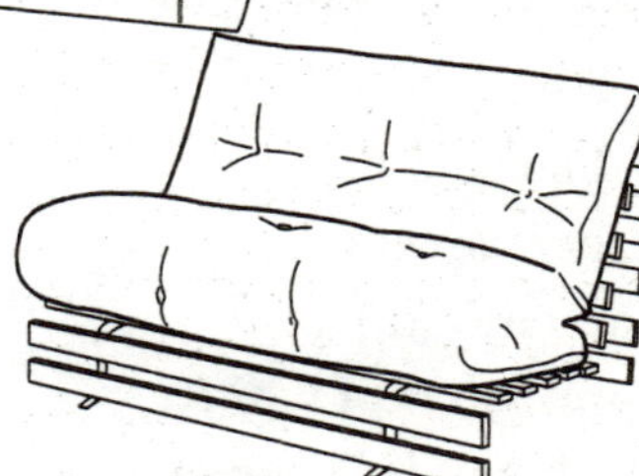

sofá-cama (sofa-bed)

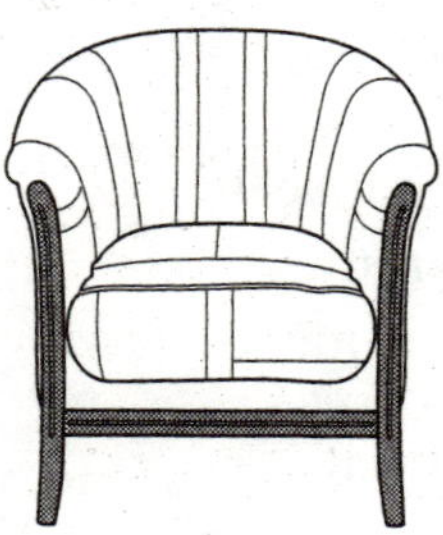

butaca (armchair)

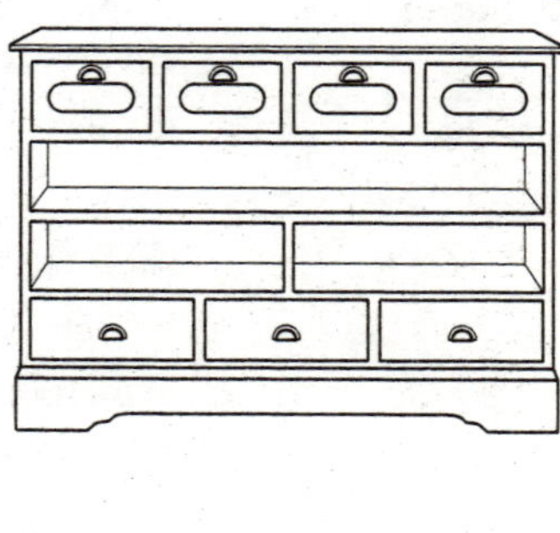

aparador (sideboard)

El dormitorio – the bedroom

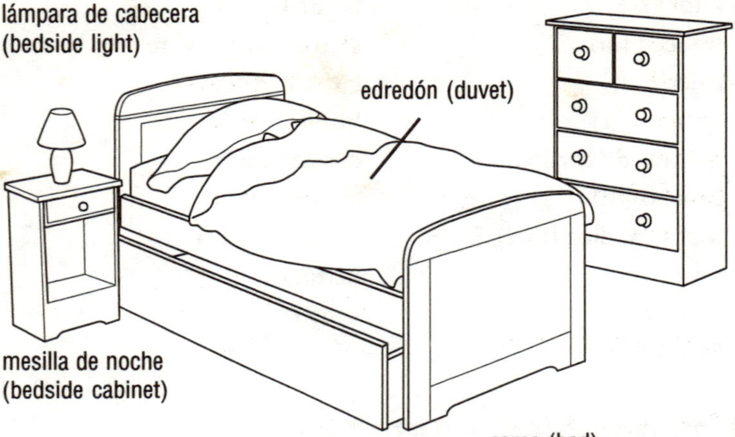

Los muebles – furniture

arcón (m)	chest
almohada (f)	pillow
aparador (m)	sideboard
armario (m)	wardrobe or cupboard
armario de TV/hi-fi	TV/hi-fi cabinet
armario de la vajilla	display cabinet for crockery / silverware
armario de vitrina	display cabinet for glassware
asiento (m)	seat
balda (f)	shelf (in cupboard)
banco (m)	bench
butaca (m)	armchair

cama (f)	bed
cama (f) de columnas	four-poster bed
cojín (m)	cushion
colchón (m)	mattress
cómoda (f)	chest of drawers
consola (f)	small cabinet
edredón (m)	duvet
estantería (f)	set of shelves
estantería de libros	bookcase
juego (m) de...	set of, e.g. *juego de 2 almohadas* = set of 2 pillows
lámpara de cabecera (f)	bedside light
litera (f)	bunk bed
mesa (f)	table
mesa (f) de centro	coffee table
mesilla (f) de noche	bed side cabinet
mimbre (m)	cane, rattan
silla (f)	chair
sillón (m)	easy chair
sofá (m)	sofa
sofá-cama (m)	sofa-bed
tocador (m)	dressing table
tresillo (m)	3-piece sofa suite
vitrina (f)	showcase

English–Spanish quick reference

Paint – la pintura

brush	brocha (f), pincel (m)
dust sheet	sábana (f)
gloss	brillante
house paint	pintura (f) para fachadas
masking tape	cinta (f) de enmascarar
non-drip	anti-goteo

one-coat	monocapa
paint tray	cubeta (f) de pintura
primer	pintura (f) de imprimación
rag	trapo (m)
roller	rodillo (m)
turpentine	trementina (f)
undercoat	subcapa (f)
varnish	barniz (m)
wood stain	tinte (m) para madera

Wall coverings – los revestimientos de paredes

cork tile	placa (f)/plancha (f) de corcho
filling knife	espátula (f)
lining paper	papel (m) para forrar
measuring tape	cinta métrica (m)
paper stripper	raspador (m) de papel pintado
pasting brush	brocha (f) de encolar
pasting table	mesa (f) de encolar
plumb line	plomada (f)
scissors	tijera (f)
seam roller	rodillo (m) de junturas
spirit level	nivel (m) de burbuja
sponge	esponja (f)
Stanley knife	cutter (m)/cortador universal (m)
string	cordel (m)
textile	tejido (m)
vinyl wallpaper	papel (m) pintado vinílico
wallpaper	papel pintado (m)
wallpaper brush	brocha (f) de empapelador
wallpaper paste	cola (f) para papel pintado
wallpaper, ready-pasted	papel preencolado (m)
wallpaper smoother	alisador (m)

Tiling – el alicatado

ceramic tile	azulejo cerámico (m)
floor tile	baldosa (f)
glue spreader	espátula dentada (f)
mirror tile	azulejo espejado (m)
tile (floor)	baldosa (f)
tile (wall)	azulejo (m)
tile cement	cemento cola (m)
tile cutter	cortador (m) de baldosas
tile pincers	tenazas (fpl) de alicatado

Floor coverings – los revestimientos de suelos

carpet	moqueta (f)
carpet/lino tile	loseta (f) de moqueta/de vinilo
laminate flooring	parqué (m) en paneles
parquet	parqué inglés (m)
rug	alfombra (f)
vinyl flooring	vinilo (m)
wood flooring	parqué (m), tarima flotante (f)
wood mosaic flooring	parqué mosaico (m)

Curtains and blinds – las cortinas y los estores

blind	estor (m), persiana (f)
curtain	cortina (f)
curtain hook	ganchos (m)
curtain pelmet	galería (f)
curtain rod	barra de cortina (f)
curtain runners	topes rodillos (mpl)
curtain tape	cinta (f) de frunciso
curtain track	riel (m) de cortinas
net curtains	visillo (m)
netting	tul (m)
venetian blind	veneciana (f)

Furniture – los muebles

armchair	butaca (f)
bed	cama (f)
bedside light	lámpara (f) de cabecera
bedside table	mesilla de noche (f)
bench	banco (m)
bookcase	estantería (f) de libros
chair	silla (f)
chest	arcón (m)
chest of drawers	cómoda (f)
coffee table	mesa (f) de centro
cupboard	armario (m)
cushion	cojín (m)
dressing table	tocador (m)
duvet	edredón (m)
easy chair	sillón (m)
mattress	colchón (m)
pillow	almohada (f)
seat	asiento (m)
set of shelves	estantería (f)
sideboard	aparador (m)
sofa	sofá (m)
sofa-bed	sofá-cama (m)
table	mesa (f)
TV/hi-fi cabinet	armario(m) de TV/hi-fi
wardrobe	armario (m)

09 el jardín – the garden

Almost the same...

The Spanish love to make jokes about the Englishman and his lawn, but if you find yourself the butt of such hilarity, don't take it personally – they have an odd sense of humour (they find Benny Hill incredibly funny...). However stiff your upper lip, there'll be no English garden here. Spain has a different climate, a different eco-system – and a different approach to gardens.

In much of Spain it's too hot and dry to keep a lawn green through the summer without regular watering. If you don't have your own spring or well, you will pay for every drop of water used by the *aspersor* (sprinkler) – assuming you're allowed to use it. There are often hosepipe bans during dry spells. And will you be there to water it and cut it? If not, who will look after it for you, and at what cost? If your home is in an *urbanización*, this won't present a real problem – communal garden areas will be tended by contractors under the terms of your service charge. The only thing you'll need to worry about is looking after your pot plants, which can be hooked up to a *kit de riego semi-automático* – a big container of water with spidery hosepipes running off to all your pots, keeping them drip-fed until you come back.

For those of you who want more greenery in your garden, ask yourself what you want it to do for you, and what your limitations are. Is it ornamental or do you want to be able to add ice and a slice of your own lemons to your afternoon *copa* (drink)? What's the temperature range in your area? How much of the year are you going to spend there, and is there anyone nearby who you can persuade to pop over and do some watering now and then? Peer over the fence and see how your neighbours use their gardens. What are they growing? You may be able to do more than you think, even if you're not there to water and weed regularly. Some fruit trees survive remarkably well in poor, dry soil and still produce a lovely crop – the *almendro* (almond) or *olivo* (olive) for instance, or perhaps a citrus tree – a *naranjo* (orange) or a *limonero* (lemon). How about a *vid* (grape vine)?

For most Brits in Spain, the most important parts of the garden are not the lawn and the veg plot, but the swimming pool and the patio. Lazy afternoons by the pool and summer evenings sipping a nice cold *copa* and eating olives on the patio with friends. Isn't that why you bought the place?

Check at the ayuntamiento

- Walls, fences and outbuildings may be subject to planning controls.
- A swimming pool will also need planning approval – and may well increase your local taxes.

Los muros, las vallas y los cercos – walls, fences and hedges

If you have bought a plot of land, the only thing marking it off from your neighbours may be a line in the sand (literally). While we're all for being friendly with the people next door, you will probably want something more substantial than that. As a general rule, you can create any kind of enclosure up to 2 m high without planning permission, but there are exceptions.

The best way to start – as always – it to look around you. What do the locals have around their properties? Would this suit you? If so, you can almost certainly go ahead without worrying. If you want to build something that is very different, go and talk to the *ayuntamiento* first.

balaustrada (f)	stone balustrade
bambú (m)	bamboo
cerco (m)	fence/hedge
cerco vivo (m)	hedge (literally 'living fence')
larguero (m)	rail of fence
listón (m)	fence post
malla (f)	mesh fencing
muro (m)	wall (stone)
panel (m) de valla	fencing panel
panel (m) paravista	latticed fencing panel
seto (m)	hedge
valla (f)	fence
verja (f)	gate

Las dependencias – outbuildings

When planning outbuildings, if they are anything more than a big dog kennel or a small tool store – permission is probably needed. You must submit a *declaración de obras* (notice of works), and possibly a *licencia de obras* (building permit).

La piscina – the swimming pool

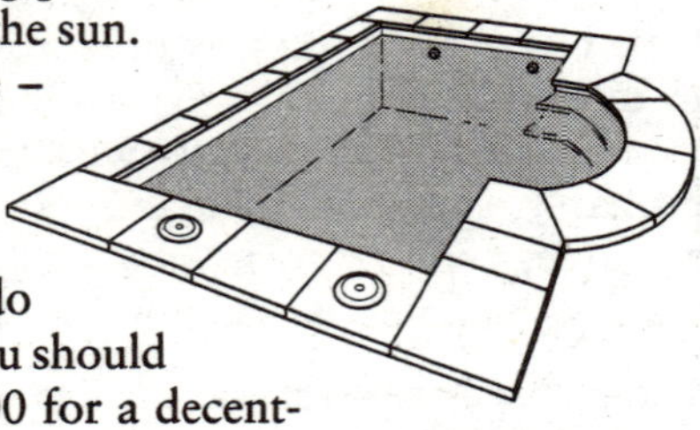

For many people, a swimming pool is an essential part of any home in the sun. Installing one is quite simple – just decide how big it should be, where it should go and how much you are willing to pay and get a professional to do the job! It won't be cheap – you should expect to pay at least €15,000 for a decent-sized pool – and it will need regular maintenance, which will take time and money. But the pool will add value to the house, if you ever come to resell it, and you cannot put a price on the pleasure it will give to you and your guests.

Some things to consider when planning your pool – discuss these with the pool builder:

- Should you opt for a salt water pool? Salt water discourages algae and needs lower chlorine levels, but can corrode metal pipes and machinery.
- What kind of summer and winter covers will the pool need? Can you haul a plastic cover off by hand or do you need to fit a roller? How about a *cubierta telescópica* – a glazed roof on runners which slides open or closed as needed?
- Where will the pump and filtration unit go? Is there a convenient spot in the outbuildings or do you need a pump house?
- How big, and what shape? Curved pools are more expensive but are easier to clean – no corners to stymie robot cleaners.
- Do you want a pre-formed pool liner or a custom-made concrete structure? What will you cover it with – pool paint, ceramic tiles or mosaic?

The cost of a pool can vary enormously, so many of these questions are best left until you've answered the first and most important ones: what's your *presupuesto* (budget)? Who will use it, for what, and how often?

Make sure you or your builders get a *licencia de obras* (building permit) for the pool – unless it's a *piscina desmontable* (above-ground temporary pool). If you get your pool builders involved early in the process, they can guide you through the paperwork, or handle it for you.

If you construct a fixed pool, you must inform the local *oficina de hacienda* (tax office), as it will affect your local property taxes.

Hang about lads... IVA an idea!

If you are buying a new build property, it is cheaper to have the pool built now than later. Building work normally incurs *IVA* (VAT) at 16%, but new build work – including the pool – is only taxed at 7%.

antialgas (m)	anti-algal product
azulejos (mpl)	tiles
bomba (f)	pump
borde (m)	edge of pool
cerco (m) de protección	safety fence
cloro (m)	chlorine
cubierta (f)	cover
depuradora (f)	purification unit
escalera (f)	steps
filtro (m) de arena	sand filter
mosaico (m)	mosaic tiling
limpiafondos automático (m)	robot pool cleaner
liner (m)	pool liner
pavimento (m) de madera	decking
pintura (f) para piscinas	pool-lining paint
piscina (f) de hormigón	concrete-built pool
piscina (f) desmontable	temporary pool

piscina prefabricada (f)	moulded pool liner
presupuesto (m)	budget, or quote
robot limpiador de piscina (m)	pool cleaning robot
tratamientos químicos (mpl)	chemical treatments
vaso de piscina prefabricado	moulded pool liner

Pool robots come in weird and wonderful shapes, but all work in much the same way. They are powered by the main pump and wander across the bottom and up the sides, dislodging and hoovering up sediment.

Los muebles del jardín – garden furniture

tumbona (sun bed)

silla plegable (folding chair)

mesa plegable (folding table)

calefactor de patio (patio heater)

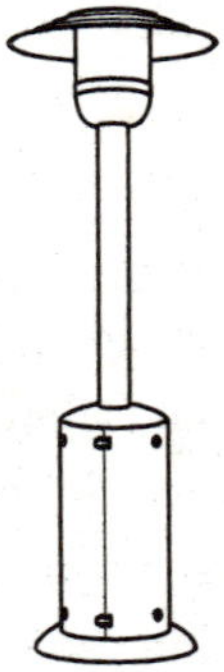

carrito (bar trolley)

aluminio (m)	aluminium
antorcha (f)	garden flare
balancín (m)	swing seat

barbacoa (f)	barbeque
cajón (m) de arena	sand pit
calefactor (m) de patio	patio heater
carrito (m)	bar trolley
cojín (m)	cushion
colchón (m) de tumbona	mattress (for sun bed)
hamaca (f)	hammock, but can also mean 'deck chair'
hierro (m) fundido	cast iron
luz (f) de jardín	garden light
parrilla (f)	barbeque
silla (f) plegable	folding chair
sombrilla (f)	sunshade/parasol
tumbona (f)	sun bed/deck chair

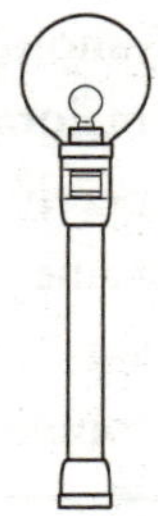

A *luz de energía solar* stores electricity during the day and then switches on at dusk to shine all night.

La jardinería – gardening

Garden centres are not as common in Spain as they are in the UK – traditionally, urbanites live in garden-less apartments, while in the countryside cultivating land is a job, not a hobby. However, enough people have small gardens or extensive pot plant collections these days, so you should be able to find somewhere which stocks plants and seeds, pots, composts, tools and so on.

- The larger *bricolajes* (DIY stores) usually have a gardening section, as do the large *supermercados* like Carrefour and Alcampo.
- In rural areas there are agricultural retailers who also handle gardening supplies. These can be very good value.
- If you want trees and shrubs, go to the *semillero* (nursery).

Hierbabuena and hierbas malas

La hierba means 'grass', but in some form or another can refer to pretty much anything small and green. *Hierbas aromáticas* are cooking herbs, *hierbas malas* ('bad herbs') are weeds, and *hierbabuena* ('good herb') is mint. I've no idea why mint is singled out for sainthood among herbs – just one of those things.

albahaca (f)	basil
cebollinos (mpl)	chives
cilantro (m)	coriander
eneldo (m)	dill
hierbabuena (f)	mint
hinojo (m)	fennel
mejorana (f)	marjoram
perejil (m)	parsley
romero (m)	rosemary
salvia (f)	sage
tomillo (m)	thyme

Water, water, nowhere...

Given the arid summers in many parts of Spain, there are plenty of ingenious water-efficient devices for watering on the market. Go for *riego subterráneo* (porous underground pipes) or *riego por goteo* (drip watering) systems, and make sure they're *automático* if you're not around much. Many systems come with a *sensor de lluvia* (rain sensor) which cuts off the water supply when it's not needed.

Las herramientas – tools

abono (m)	fertiliser
aspersor (m)	sprinkler
bidón (m)	water barrel
carretilla (f)	wheelbarrow
césped (m)	lawn
cobertizo (m)	garden shed
cortacésped (m)	mower

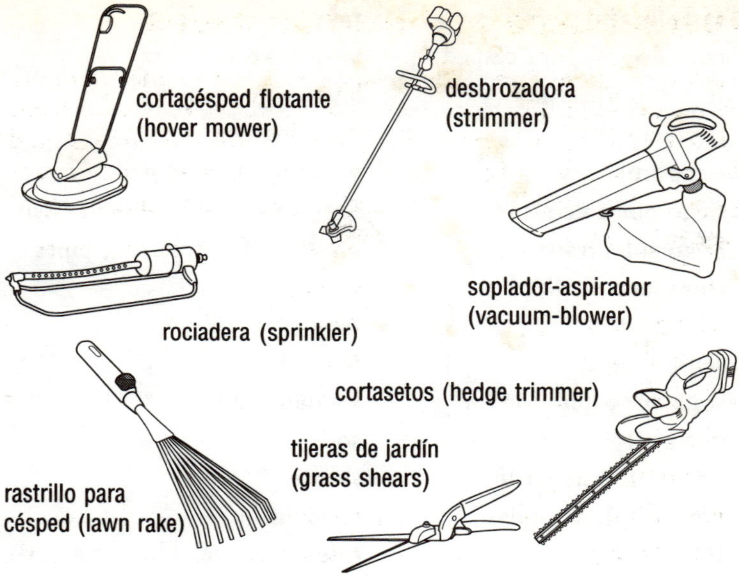

cortacésped flotante (m)	hover mower
cortasetos (m)	hedge trimmer
desbrozadora (f)	strimmer
desplantador (m)	potting trowel
enrollador (m)	roller for hosepipe
escarifadora (f)	scarifier
escoba (f) de jardín	garden brush
estanque (m)	pond
extensión (f)	extension lead
fuente (f)	fountain
horca (f)	gardening fork
incinerador (m)	incinerator
invernadero (m)	greenhouse
jardinera (f)	planter (rectangular pot)
maceta (f)	pot
manguera (f)	hose
motosierra (f)	chain saw
pala (f)	spade
picadora (f)	shredder

rastrillo (m)	rake
rastrillo (m) para césped	lawn rake
recortabordes (m)	lawn edge trimmer
regadera (f)	watering can
riego (m)	watering, irrigation
riego por goteo (m)	drop-by-drop watering system
riego subterráneo (m)	underground watering pipes
rociadera (f)	sprinkler
semilla (f)	seed
sensor (m) de lluvia	rain sensor
soplador-aspirador (m)	vacuum-blower
tierra (f)	soil
tijeras (fpl) de jardín	shears
tijeras (fpl) de podar	secateurs
tractorcito (m)	ride-on mower ('little tractor')

English–Spanish quick reference

Walls, fences and hedges – los muros, las vallas y los setos

fence	valla (f), cerco (m)
fencing panel	panel (m) de valla
gate	portal (m)
hedge	seto (m), cerco vivo (m)
mesh fencing	malla (f)
wall	muro (m)

Swimming pool – la piscina

chlorine	cloro (m)
cover	cubierta (f)
decking	pavimento (m) de madera
edge of pool	borde (m)
mosaic tiling	mosaico (m)
pool liner, moulded	vaso (m) de piscina prefabricado

pool liner, sheet	liner (m)
pool paint	pintura (f) para piscinas
pump	bomba (f)
safety fence	cerco (m) de protección
sand filter	filtro (m) de arena
steps	escalera (f)
tiles	azulejos (mpl)

Garden furniture – los muebles del jardín

aluminium	aluminio (m)
bar trolley	carrito (m)
cushion	cojín (m)
deck chair	tumbona (f)/hamaca (f)
flare	antorcha (f)
folding	plegable
garden light	luz (f) de jardín
mattress (for sun bed)	colchón (m) de tumbona
patio heater	calefactor (m) de patio
sand pit	cajón (m) de arena
sun bed	tumbona (f)
swing seat	balancín (m)

Cooking herbs – las hierbas aromáticas

basil	albahaca (f)
chives	cebollinos (mpl)
coriander	cilantro (m)
dill	eneldo (m)
fennel	hinojo (m)
marjoram	mejorana (f)
mint	hierbabuena (f)
parsley	perejil (m)
rosemary	romero (m)
sage	salvia (f)
thyme	tomillo (m)

Gardening – la jardinería

extension lead	extensión (f)
fertiliser	abono (m)
fountain	fuente (f)
garden brush	escoba (f) de jardín
garden shed	cobertizo (m)
gardening fork	horca (f)
grape vine	vid (f)
hedge trimmer	cortasetos (m)
hose	manguera (f)
hover mower	cortacésped flotante (m)
incinerator	incinerador (m)
lawn	césped (m)
lawn rake	rastrillo (m) para céspedes
lemon tree	limonero (m)
mower	cortacésped (m)
olive tree	olivo (m)
orange tree	naranjo (m)
planter	jardinera (f)
pot	maceta (f)
potting trowel	desplantador (m)
rake	rastrillo (m)
ride-on mower	tractorcito (m)
roller (for hosepipe)	enrollador (m)
seed	semilla (f)
shears	tijeras (fpl) de jardín
shredder	picadora (f)
soil	tierra (f)
spade	pala (f)
sprinkler	aspersor (m)/rociadera (f)
strimmer	desbrozadora (f)
vacuum-blower	soplador-aspirador (m)
water barrel	bidón (m)
wheelbarrow	carretilla (f)

10 una hora de español – an hour of Spanish

The CD and the book

This chapter and the CD are built around the same sets of words, and should be used together. The CD gives practice in speaking and listening; the book links the written to the spoken word.

The aim of this chapter is not to teach you Spanish – if you want to learn the language properly, try a *Michel Thomas* course, or one of the titles in the *Teach Yourself* series, such as *Spanish* or *Instant Spanish*. The aim here is to provide you with a core of words and phrases that will help you to find what you need when you are buying, building, maintaining or equipping your Spanish home.

If you already speak Spanish to a greater or less degree, we hope that this chapter will give you a firmer grasp of those specialist words that the householder needs. Skip the rest of this section and go straight to *La búsqueda – the search* (page 162) and Track 2 on the CD.

Speaking and listening

When you speak Spanish to a native, don't try too hard to get a perfect accent. If the Spanish think that you can speak their language well, they won't make allowances when they talk to you. And you need them to make allowances! Spanish people tend to talk quickly – you need them to slow down so that you can distinguish each word or phrase from the next. Rehearse what you want to say, in your head, let it flow out smoothly, then stand there like an idiot after they reply, without a clue as to what they said. We've done this too often ourselves!

Speak slowly yourself, and let them hear from your accent that you are a foreigner, and they might speak more slowly and clearly to you. Speaking slowly is not something that comes naturally to the Spanish, so you'll probably have to ask them to slow down.

Here's your first – and most essential – Spanish phrase:

repita, y menos rápido	again and not so fast

To which you could add, politely:

por favor	please

What follows is a brief guide to basic pronunciation. Listen to the CD while you are working through this.

Speak easy

Unlike with many other languages, Spanish pronunciation is very kind to the beginner – it only has one silent letter, and letters are nearly always pronounced the same way. Once you know how each letter sounds by itself, you can say any word you can read.

There are two sounds which we don't really have in English. It will take a lot of practice to get these sounding totally native, but don't worry – pronouncing them English-style won't stop you being understood.

j is a loud aspirated 'h' made at the front of the throat. After a lifetime of smoking filterless cigarettes, a tough old Spaniard may make this sound very harsh and guttural. If you can't manage this, just make your 'h' sound as meaty as possible – slightly hissing, even. Many native speakers actually make it sound closer to a forceful 'h' than an exercise in throat-clearing.

junta	**hoonta**	join

rr – the double 'r' is rolled, with the tongue making a rapid trill against the roof of your mouth near your front teeth. Some people find this very easy, others never quite manage it – some of us can't reliably roll an rr at will after years of practice! But it's no big deal – just draw your 'r' out a little and try to make it sound as forceful as you can.

tierra	**tee-ehrrrra**	earth

Vowels

Spanish vowels always sound the same, no matter where they appear in a word, or what combination.

a is **a** as in had

casa	**cassa**	house

e is **e** as in bed. Don't be tempted to soften it at the ends of words – it's still a strong sound, almost like 'ay' as in 'pay'

metro	**metro**	metre
Alicante	**alee-can-tay**	Alicante

i is **ee** as in meet

pintar	**peentar**	to paint

o is **o** as in copper

piso	**pee-so**	apartment

u is *oo* as in move

tubo	**toobo**	tube

If two vowels appear next to each other, they are both fully pronounced, in turn.

piedra	**pee-edra**	stone
chimenea	**cheemeneya**	chimney/fireplace

Consonants

Most are pronounced as in English, but be careful not to change your pronunciation of a letter the way you might in English sometimes. For instance, 's' is pronounced like our **s** as in 'soft', never like a **z** as in 'laser'. The following letters are different:

b, *v* *b* and *v* are both pronounced the same, somewhere in between the two English sounds, but closer to 'b'. Try making a 'b' sound, but open your lips very slightly.

¡basta!	**bhasta**	enough!
volver	**bhol-bhair**	to return

c is **k** if followed by *a*, *o* or *u*

cobre	**kobray**	copper

c is a soft **th** if followed by *e* or *i*

cinta	**thinta**	tape

d is usually the same as our **d**, but when it's at the end of a word it sounds softer – more like **th** in 'with'.

Madrid	**Madreeth**	Madrid

g is a hard **g** as in 'good', except when followed by an *e* or *i*, when it is the same aspirated **h** as described above for 'j'.

agua	**agwa**	water
coger	cohair	to take/to catch

h is always **silent**

hotel	**otel**	hotel

ll is **y** as in you

valla	**vaya**	fence

ñ is **ny** as in onion

señor	**senyor**	mister

qu is just **k**, not **kw**

quince	**kinthay**	fifteen

z is a lisped s

pozo potho well/tank

Stressing out

Whenever we speak, some parts of words are stressed, or said more heavily, than others. If you get the stress wrong on a word, it won't affect the meaning, but it might make it harder for the Spanish to understand. For example, try saying the English word 'radiator' with the stress on the last syllable instead of the first: 'radia**tor**'. It may sound weird, but you'd probably understand what someone meant if if they said it to you.

It's the same in Spanish. As a rule, the second-to-last syllable of a word is the one to stress. So we have *pozo* and *chimenea*. If a word breaks this rule, it is written with an accent over the stressed syllable: *rápido*. If *rápido* didn't have the accent, it would be pronounced 'rapeedo'.

Gender and endings

All nouns are either masculine or feminine. We've neither of us ever understood why or what determines the gender of a noun (apart from the obvious ones that refer to people or animals) – or even, why they bother at all! There are a few guides as to the gender of a word. One that ends in 'a' is almost certainly feminine, as are most words ending in 'ción', and most words ending in 'o' are masculine – but that leaves an awful lot that you just have to know.

A noun's gender affects the words around it. For 'the' you use *el* if the noun is masculine and *la* if it is feminine; likewise 'a' is either *un* (m) or *una* (f). If there's more than one of them, it's *los* (mpl) or *las* (fpl) for 'the', and *unos* (mpl) or *unas* (fpl) for 'some'.

For example, *casa* (house) is feminine, and *piso* (apartment) is masculine. That gives us:

the house	*la casa*
the apartment	*el apartamento*
a house	*una casa*
an apartment	*un apartamento*
the houses	*las casas*
some apartments	*unos apartamentos*

Try not to get too hung up on the gender thing. If you talk about *el casa*, instead of *la casa*, a Spaniard will know what you mean.

Adjectives have a different ending if a noun is masculine or feminine. Usually, it's just a matter of swapping the final 'o' for an 'a'. For example, *pequeño* means 'small', so 'a small house' – which is feminine – becomes *una casa pequeña* (the adjective is usually placed after the noun). Sometimes it doesn't change at all, as with *grande* (big) for example – you can have *un piso grande* (a big apartment) or *una casa grande* (a big house).

The endings of adjectives also change with plural nouns – and usually by just adding an 's' to the end, to match the 's' on the end of the noun.

a small house	*una casa pequeña*
the small houses	*las casas pequeñas*
some big apartments	*unos pisos grandes*

Verbs

Spanish verbs 'conjugate'. Their endings, and sometimes the whole word, change depending upon who is doing the thing and when they are doing it. Verbs also conjugate in English, but not as much.

For example, *tomar* means 'to take'. Here's how it conjugates:

yo tomo	I take
tú tomas	you (singular, informal) take
usted toma	you (singular, formal) take
él toma	he takes
ella toma	she takes
nosotros tomamos	we take
vosotros tomáis	you (plural, informal) take
ustedes toman	you (plural, formal) take
ellos/ellas toman	they take

That may look quite intimidating, but in practice if you said *yo toma...* to a Spanish seller, they would know what you meant well enough to sell you stuff. If you ignore the informal forms of 'you', it stays fairly simple.

Tú o usted – which you?

The Spanish have four words for 'you'. *Tú* and *usted* (also written *Vd.* for short) are for when you are talking to one person, but *tú* is used with people you are familiar with, while *usted* shows more respect. *Vosotros* is the plural of *tú*, and *ustedes* (*Vds.*) is the plural of *usted.* When in doubt, use *Vd.* or *Vds.* – they're also easier when conjugating verbs!

The only thing you need to watch out for when listening to Spanish is that they often drop the personal pronouns (I, you, we, he, she, etc). Because all their verb forms sound different, they don't really need them in a sentence. When speaking yourself though, you might want to keep them in to avoid misunderstandings.

Most other verbs that end 'ar' conjugate in the same way – chop off the 'ar' or add *-a, -as, -amos* or *-an,* e.g. with *pagar* (to pay), you would say *yo pago* (I pay) or *nosotros pagamos* (we pay).

Other verbs end in 'er'. For these, we do much the same – trim the verb down to its root and add *-e, -es, -emos* or *-en*; e.g. *comer* is to eat, which gives us *él come* (he eats) and *nosotros comemos* (we eat).

Verbs ending in 'ir' are identical to 'er' verbs, except that the 'we' form ends with *-imos* instead of *-emos*; e.g. *vivir* (to live) gives us *ella vive* (she lives) and *nosotros vivimos* (we live).

Not all verbs follow the patterns exactly, and some are even more irregular. You should at least be aware of these two.

ser **– to be**

yo soy	I am
tú eres	you are
él es	he is
ella es	she is
Vd. es	you are
nosotros somos	we are
vosotros sois	you are
ellos/ellas son	they are
Vds. son	you are

ir – to go

yo voy	I go
tú vas	you go
él/ella/Vd. va	he/she goes, you go
nosotros vamos	we go
vosotros vais	you go
ellos/ellas/Vds. van	they/you go

We've only looked at the present tense. There are also several ways of talking about past and future events, all of which affect the shape and sound of the verb. And there is no single pattern to the way they conjugate, even for the 'regular' verbs. Take our advice – live in the present, never write anything down, and just chop off the ending of the verb and add *-amos* for *nosotros, -o* for *yo,* and *-a* for everything else. It's not perfect, but you'll get by and you will amuse the locals. When they've stopped laughing, they'll be pleased to help you – at least you're trying, which is more than can be said of many of our fellow Brits abroad.

ser y estar – to be or to be!

Another thing which can cause confusion is that the Spanish also have two words for 'to be'. *Ser* is used mainly to describe permanent properties of a thing, e.g. *La casa es preciosa* (the house is lovely). *Estar* is used mainly in relation to position, e.g. *El piso está cerca del mar* (the apartment is near the sea). It won't matter much if you get it wrong yourself, but it's good to be aware of when you hear other people using *ser* or *estar*.

no... – not

To say 'not' you just need to add 'no' before the verb. For example:

I am not...	*yo no soy...*

Here's a 'not' phrase you may find very useful.

I do not understand	*no entiendo*

If you want to say 'not' without a verb, it's the same word:

not many	*no mucho*

'This house sells itself'

In Chapter 1 we came across the expression *se vende esta casa*, meaning 'this house is for sale'. In fact, the literal translation is 'this house sells itself'. Some common phrases you'll meet in this book use this kind of structure. For example:

Where can I find a notary?	*¿dónde se puede encontrar un notario?*

Literally, this means 'where can a notary find himself?' – 'where can a notary be found? Notice that written questions have an upside-down question mark at the start as well as the normal one at the end.

Do you sell nails?	*¿se venden aquí clavos?*

Literally: 'do nails sell themselves here?'

Notice that the verb in these sentences does not refer to the 'I' or 'you' in the English, but to the thing you are looking for. This means it has to change for singular and plural objects:

Where can I find a hammer?	*¿dónde se puede encontrar un martillo?*
Where can I find the screws?	*¿dónde se pueden encontrar los tornillos?*

Don't get hung up on matching the verb perfectly – if you say *¿se vende aquí los clavos?*, nobody's going to mind!

Greetings

hello, literally 'good day'	buenos días
good evening	buenas tardes
goodbye (for now)	hasta luego
goodbye (for a while)	adiós
thank you	gracias
thank you very much	muchas gracias
don't mention it	no hay de qué
pardon me	perdona
how do you do?	¿qué tal?
fine, thanks	bien, gracias
I am called...	me llamo...

Asking questions

To form a question, just say it as if it was a statement, but with a rising inflection:

do you speak English?	*¿usted habla inglés?*
is the house pretty?	*¿la casa es bonita?*

Questions mainly use the same order as in English, but they don't switch the verb and subject over as often as we do. The subject (the house) usually comes before the verb (is).

Useful question words are *quién* (who), *dónde* (where), *qué* (which), *cuándo* (when), *cómo* (how) and *por qué* (why).

where is the town hall?	¿dónde está el ayuntamiento?
it's to the right	está a la derecha
it's to the left	está a la izquierda
go straight on	todo recto
it's over there	está allá
it's here	está aquí
how much is it?	¿cuánto es?

Los números – numbers

0	cero	15	quince	60	sesenta
1	uno	16	dieciséis	70	setenta
2	dos	17	diecisiete	80	ochenta
3	tres	18	dieciocho	90	noventa
4	cuatro	19	diecinueve	100	cien
5	cinco	20	veinte	200	doscientos
6	seis	21	veintiuno	300	trescientos
7	siete	22	veintidós	400	cuatrocientos
8	ocho	...	etc	but notice	
9	nueve	30	treinta	500	quinientos
10	diez	31	treinta y uno	600	seiscientos
11	once	32	treinta y dos		
12	doce	...	etc	1000	mil
13	trece	40	cuarenta	2 000	dos mil
14	catorce	50	cincuenta	1 000 000	un millón

why?	¿por qué?
this house is cheap, why?	esta casa es barata, ¿por qué?
why is this house so dear?	¿por qué esta casa es tan cara?
how old is this apartment?	¿cuantos años tiene este piso?
what time is it?	¿qué hora es?
it is 7 o'clock	son las siete
half past eight	son las ocho y media
quarter to ten	diez menos quarto
at five pm	a las cinco de la tarde
at nine am	a las nueve de la mañana
it's dinner time	es la hora de comer
when?, at what time?	¿a qué hora?
on what day?	¿qué día?
what date?	¿qué fecha?
can we set a date?	¿podemos fijar una cita?

Las fechas – dates

Los días – the days

Sunday	domingo
Monday	lunes
Tuesday	martes
Wednesday	miércoles
Thursday	jueves
Friday	viernes
Saturday	sábado
tomorrow	mañana
today	hoy
yesterday	ayer

Los meses – the months

January	enero
February	febrero
March	marzo
April	abril
May	mayo
June	junio
July	julio
August	agosto
September	septiembre
October	octubre
November	noviembre
December	diciembre

La búsqueda – the search (Track 2)

Let's start with some words and phrases to help you find that house.

I am looking for...	(yo) busco...
we are looking for...	(nosotros) buscamos...
I want to buy...	(yo) quiero comprar...
we want to buy...	(nosotros) queremos comprar...
...a small apartment	...un piso pequeño
...a large apartment	...un piso grande
...a house	...una casa
...in the town	...en la ciudad
...in the country	...una finca rústica
...to restore	...para renovar
...in good condition	...en buen estado
is this house for sale?	¿se vende esta casa?

Defining the house

Three key ways to define a house are its size – measured in square metres of floor space – the number of rooms and its price. You'll need to brush up your numbers for all of these. But if you want to make sure that you've understood the numbers correctly, ask the agents to write them down. Figures don't need translation!

about	alrededor de
more than	más de
less than	menos de
50 m^2 (cottage size)	cincuenta metros cuadrados
100 m^2 (average UK semi)	cien metros cuadrados
200 m^2 (large detached)	doscientos metros cuadrados
two bedrooms	dos habitaciones
five rooms	cinco cuartos
€60 000	sesenta mil euros
€120 000	ciento veinte mil euros
€1 000 000	un millón de euros

The features

What features are essential, desirable or to be avoided?

there must be...	tiene que tener...
does it have...	tiene...
is there the possibility of...	hay posibilidad de...
...a kitchen	...una cocina
...a bathroom	...un cuarto de baño
...a swimming pool	...una piscina
...a garden	...un jardín
...a attic	...un desván
...a cellar	...una bodega
...a beautiful view	...buenas vistas
does it need work?	¿necesita mejoras?
is it on the mains drains?	¿está conectado al alcantarillado?
is the roof in a good state?	¿el techo está en buen estado?

Your decision

And what do you think of the property? Do you want to keep looking or is it time to start negotiating the price?

no, thank you	no, gracias
it's too dear	es demasiado caro
it's too big	es demasiado grande
it's too small	es demasiado pequeño
there is too much to do	necesita demasiadas mejoras
perhaps	quizás
I have other houses to see	tengo que ver otras casas
do you have other houses?	¿Vd. tiene otras casas?
I like this house...	me gusta esta casa...
we like this house...	nos gusta esta casa...
...but not the price	...pero no el precio
can we negotiate?	¿podemos negociar?
here is my offer	aquí tiene mi oferta

it's perfect!	¡es perfecto!
agreed	de acuerdo

La venta – the sale (Track 3)

There is not enough in this book to enable you to handle safely the legal and financial aspects of house purchase. You must have a good grasp of Spanish – and of Spanish law – or the services of a translator and/or English-speaking lawyer.

Before you commit yourself to the purchase, you may want to check the price, or the cost – and feasibility – of essential works.

could you recommend...	¿Vd. puede recomendar...
...an architect?	...un arquitecto?
...a notary?	...un notario?
I need/we need...	necesito/necesitamos...
...a valuation...	...una valoración...
...an estimate...	...un presupuesto...
...for this house	...para esta casa

(There is more on estimates in the next section, *Las obras – building work*, Track 4.)

You might want to find out the level of the local taxes and/or the service charges in an apartment block, and you should also check who's paying the agent's fees.

where is the town hall?	¿dónde está el ayuntamiento?
where is the tax office?	¿dónde está la Oficina Liquidadora?
how much are...?	¿cuántos son...
...the taxes for this address	...los impuestos para esta dirección?
...the service charges	...los gastos de comunidad?
who pays the agency fees?	¿quién paga las comisiones de la agencia?
the seller pays them	el vendedor las paga

With your queries answered, you should be ready to commit, though there may be conditions in some cases.

we are ready to buy	estamos listos a comprar
I want to buy this house...	quiero comprar esta casa...
...at the price of...€ 000	...al precio de...mil euros
...under these conditions	...con estas condiciones
the town planning search must be satisfactory	el informe urbanístico tiene que ser satisfactorio
I must get a mortgage	tengo que obtener una hipoteca
I would like to see the electrical safety certificate	quisiera ver el boletín de instalación eléctrica
I can't pay the deposit today	no puedo pagar la fianza hoy
I will transfer the money from the UK	haré una transferencia desde el Reino Unido

If you want to clarify any points of the sale agreement, or set up a Spanish will, you will need to visit the *notario*.

where is the notary's office?	¿dónde está la oficina del notario?
do you speak English?	¿Vd. habla inglés?
I would like to make a will	quisiera redactar un testamento

If they are present, get the water, gas, electricity and telephone accounts transferred to your name at the time of the sale. Ask the *agencia inmobiliaria*.

does it have mains...	¿hay alimentación de...
... water?	...agua?
...gas?	...gas?
...electricity?	...electricidad?
Please transfer the accounts	Por favor, transfiera las cuentas
what time do we put the rubbish out?	¿a qué hora se saca la basura?
where is the recycling centre?	¿dónde está el centro de reciclaje?

And don't forget the *por favor* when you ask a question, or the *gracias* when you get a reply. The Spanish don't use either as much as we do, but it doesn't hurt.

Las obras – building work (Track 4)

As long as you hold your meetings on site, armed with a *dibujo* (sketch) or *plano* (plan), you can get a long way with a limited vocabulary and lots of hand waving. First find your workforce. Ask your neighbours or at the *ayuntamiento*.

can you recommend...	¿puede Vd. recomendar...
...an architect?	...un arquitecto?
...a builder?	...un albañil?
...a (structural) carpenter?	...un carpintero (de armar)?
...a roofer?	...un tejador?
...a plumber?	...un fontanero?
...an electrician?	...un electricista?
...a plasterer?	...un enyesador?

Then specify the job on site. Notice that the word for 'new' is *nuevo* if the noun is masculine, or *nueva* if it is feminine.

here are my sketch and plan	aquí tiene mi dibujo y mi plano
I want...	quiero...
...to knock down the walls	...derrumbar las paredes
...to knock down these outbuildings	...demolir estas dependencias
...to make two rooms	...crear dos habitaciones
the house needs...	la casa necesita...
...a new roof	...un tejado nuevo
...a new floor	...un solado nuevo
I want to build...	quiero construir...
...a new bathroom	...un cuarto de baño nuevo
...a new kitchen	...una cocina nueva
...an extra bedroom	...una habitación más
...a garage	...un garaje
...a swimming pool	...una piscina
this big (with gestures!)	así de grande
this high	así de altura
can you give me an estimate for this work?	¿me puede dar un presupuesto para estas obras?

when could you do it?	¿cuándo las puede hacer?

Do you need planning permission or approval of the work?

can I see the PGOU for this address?	¿puedo ver el Plan General de Ordenación Urbana para esta dirección?
could you give me...	por favour, déme...
...the address of the town hall	...la dirección del ayuntamiento
...a form for...	...un formulario para...
...planning permission	...una licencia de obras
...permission to demolish	...una licencia de demolición

La estructura – the structure

Talking to el albañil – the builder (Track 5)

can you build...	¿puede Vd. construir...
...a brick wall here?	...un muro de ladrillos aquí?
...a partition wall over there?	...un tabique allá?
...a stone chimney?	...una chimenea de piedra?
...a reinforced concrete floor?	...un solado de hormigón armado?
can you...	¿Vd. puede...
...repoint the walls?	...rejuntar los muros?
...strengthen the foundations?	...fortalecer los cimientos?
there is rising damp	hay humedad en las paredes
the house needs a damp course	la casa necesita un aislante hidrófugo

Finding tools and materials at the bricolaje (Track 6)

where can I find...	¿dónde se puede (singular)/ se pueden (plural) encontrar...
...builder's tools	...las herramientas de albañil?
...a bucket	...un balde?
...a filling knife	...una cuchilla de enlucir?
...a shavehook	...un rascador?

...a spade	...una pala?
...a spirit level	...un nivel de agua?
...a trowel	...una paleta?
...breeze blocks	...los bloques de hormigón?
...bricks	...los ladrillos?
...insulation panels	...los paneles aislantes?
...plaster blocks	...los bloques de yeso?
...cement	...el cemento?
...a lintel	...un dintel?
...plasterboard	...un panel de escayola?
...sand	...la arena?
...stones	...las piedras?
...wall ties	...los anclajes de muro?
...treatment for mould	...los productos contra el moho?
where can I hire a concrete mixer?	¿dónde se puede alquilar una hormigonera?

Talking to el carpintero – the carpenter and el tejador – the roofer (Track 7)

I would like to...	quisiera...
...create a terrace roof	...construir una terraza en el techo
can you build...	¿Vd. puede construir...
...a dormer window	...una buhardilla?
...a lathe and plaster ceiling	...un techo de varilla enlucida de yeso?
can you install...	¿Vd. puede instalar...
...a skylight	...un vélux?
...lining felt	...el cartón alquitranado?
...insulation	...el aislante?
can you renovate...	¿Vd. puede renovar...
...these rafters	...estas correas?
...the joists	...las vigas?
...the roof trusses	...la armadura del tejado?

...a hip roof	...un tejado a cuatro aguas?
...the lathing	...la varilla?
...the guttering	...los canalones?
in oak or pine?	¿en roble o en pino?
a roof of...	un tejado de...
...flat tiles	...tejas planas
...curved tiles	...tejas curvas
...slates	...pizarra
...thatch	...paja

La carpintería – woodwork

Talking to el carpintero – the joiner (Track 8)

here, we would like...	aquí, queremos...
...a built-in cupboard	...un armario empotrado
...a door	...una puerta
...wood panelling	...un machihembrado
there, we would like...	allá, queremos...
...three shelves	...tres estantes
...wood flooring	...un solado parqué
...a letter box	...un buzón
can you make...	¿Vd. puede fabricar...
...a French window	...una puerta-ventana?
...a skylight	...una claraboya?
...new shutters	...unas contraventanas nuevas?
...a roller shutter	...una persiana enrollable?
...a slatted shutter	...una persiana?
...a spiral staircase	...una escalera de caracol?
...a new handrail	...un pasamanos nuevo?
...a set of bookshelves	...una estantería de libros?

Finding materials at the bricolaje (Track 9)

where can I find...	¿dónde se puede(n) encontrar...
...chipboard	...los tableros aglomerados?

...hardboard	...los tableros de fibra dura?
...melamine panels	...los tableros laminados?
...veneer	...el rechapado?
...hardwood	...la madera frondosa?
...plywood	...los tableros contrachapados?
...tongue and grooved wood	...madera con ranuras y lengüetas?
...veneered panels	...los tableros rechapados?
...wood panels	...los tableros de madera?
...hardware for doors	...los herrajes para puertas?
...bolts	...los cerrojos?
...cylinder locks	...las cerraduras de cilindro?
...door handles	...los tiradores de puerta?
...hinges	...las bisagras?
...split hinges	...los goznes?
...mortice locks	...las cerraduras para encastrar?
...shutter catches	...los pestillos para contraventanas?
...shutter fastenings	...las fallebas?

Finding tools at the bricolaje (Track 10)

where are the wood tools?	¿dónde están las herramientas de carpintería?
do you sell ...	¿se vende(n) aquí...
...sandpaper	...papel de lija?
...chisels	...cinceles?
...cutters (Stanley knife)	...los cortadores universales?
...drill bits	...las brocas?
...electric drills	...las taladradoras eléctricas?
...jig saws	...las sierras de vaivén?
...electric screwdrivers	...los destornilladores eléctricos?
...hammers	...los martillos?
...nails	...los clavos?

...pincers	...las tenazas?
...saws	...las sierras?
...screws	...los tornillos?
...screwdrivers	...los destornilladores?
...tape measures	...los cintas métricas?
...wood glue	...la cola para madera?

La fontanería – plumbing

Talking to el fontanero – the plumber (Track 11)

can you install...	¿Vd. puede instalar...
...gutters	...los canalones?
...some copper pipes	...la tubería de cobre?
...a waste water system	...la tubería de desagüe?
...a new joint	...una juntura nueva?
...a bath and basin	...una bañera y un lavabo?
...a WC	...un inodoro?
...a septic tank	...un pozo séptico?
...a soakaway	...la tubería de drenaje?
...a soil pipe	...la tubería de esgoto?
where is...	¿dónde está...
...the stop cock	...la llave de paso?
...the drain cock	...el grifo de desagüe?
...the regulator	...el reductor de presión?
...the water meter	...el contador?
do you know someone who can empty the septic tank?	¿Vd. sabe quién puede vaciar el pozo séptico?

Shopping for bathroom and kitchen equipment (Track 12)

where can I buy...	¿dónde se puede(n) comprar...
...basins	...los lavabos?
...bathtubs	...las bañeras?
...medicine cabinets	...los armarios de medicinas?

...mirrors	...los espejos?
...a mixer tap	...un grifo monobloc?
...a plug	...un tapón?
...a rubbish bin	...un cubo de basura?
...showers	...las duchas?
...taps	...los grifos?
...towel rails	...los toalleros?
...a washer	...las arandelas?
...kitchen equipment	...los aparatos de cocina?
...a bowl	...un cuenco?
...a cooker hood	...una campana de ventilación?
...a dishwasher	...un lavaplatos?
...ovens	...los hornos?
...kitchen sinks	...los fregaderos?
...washing machines	...las lavadoras?
...work surfaces	...las encimeras para cocina?
I would like a sink with two bowls and one drainer	quisiera un fregadero con dos cuencos y un escurridor

Finding tools at the bricolaje (Track 13)

I am looking for...	Busco...
...a spanner	...una llave inglesa
...an adjustable spanner	...una llave ajustable
...a hacksaw	...una sierra para metales
...a pipe cutter	...un cortatubos
...a soldering lamp	...un soplete

La calefacción y la electricidad – heating and electricity

Talking to el ingeniero de calefacción – the heating engineer (Track 14)

can you install...	¿Vd. puede instalar...
...a fireplace	...una chimenea?

...a boiler	...una caldera?
...some radiators	...unos radiadores?
...a stove	...una estufa?
...central heating	...calefacción central?
where can I buy...	¿dónde se puede(n) comprar...
...coal	...carbón?
...logs	...leños?
...wood	...leña?
can you recommend a chimney sweep?	¿puede Vd. recomendar un deshollinador?

Talking to el electricista – the electrician

can you rewire the house?	¿Vd. puede renovar la instalación eléctrica?
where is/are...	¿dónde está/están...
...the mains switch	...el interruptor general?
...the meter	...el contador?
...the circuit breakers	...los cortacircuitos?
can you fit...	¿Vd. puede instalar...
...a socket here?	...una toma aquí?
...a fuse box?	...un cuadro de reparto?
...a light switch?	...un interruptor?
...a light fitting?	...un portalámparas?

Shopping for los electrodomésticos – electrical appliances (Track 15)

where can I find...	¿dónde se puede(n) encontrar...
...convector heaters	...los convectores?
...electric fires	...las chimeneas eléctricas?
...cookers	...las cocinas?
...DVD players	...los reproductores DVD?
...food processors	...los robots de cocina?
...freezers	...los congeladores?
...fridges	...los frigoríficos?
...kettles	...los hervidores?

...irons	...las planchas?
...telephones	...los teléfonos?
...TVs	...los televisores?
...flat screen TVs	...los televisores de pantalla plana?
...vacuum cleaners	...las aspiradoras?
...lights	...las lámparas?
...a ceiling light	...un plafón?
...a bedside light	...una lámpara de cabecera?
...a hanging light	...una lámpara colgante?
...a wall light	...un aplique?

La decoración – decorating

Finding materials at the bricolaje (Track 16)

where can I find...	¿dónde se puede(n) encontrar...
...paint	...la pintura?
...gloss paint	...la pintura brillante?
...masonry paint	...la pintura para fachadas?
...primer	...la pintura de imprimación?
...undercoat	...la subcapa?
...varnish	...el barniz?
...wood stain	...el tinte para madera?
do you sell...	¿se vende(n) aquí...
...wall coverings	...los revestimientos de paredes?
...textiles, for walls	...los revestimientos textiles?
...cork tiles	...las placas de corcho?
...wallpaper	...el papel pintado?
...tiles	...los azulejos?
...floor tiles	...las baldosas?
...mirror tiles	...los azulejos espejados?

Finding tools at the bricolaje (Track 17)

where can I find...	¿dónde se puede(n) encontrar...
...a measuring tape	...un metro de cinta?
...a paper stripper	...un raspador de papel pintado?
...a pasting brush	...una brocha de encolar?
...a spirit level	...un nivel de agua?
...brushes	...las brochas?
...paint trays	...las cubetas de pintura?
...rollers	...los rodillos?
...scissors	...las tijeras?
...a sponge	...una esponja?
...string	...el cordel?
...wallpaper paste	...la cola para papel pintado?
...a wallpaper brush	...una brocha para el papel pintado?
...a tile cutter	...un cortador de azulejos?

Finding floor coverings, curtains and furniture (Track 18)

do you sell...	¿se vende(n) aquí...
...carpets	...las moquetas?
...rugs	...las alfombras?
...laminate flooring	...la tarima flotante?
...vinyl flooring	...el vinilo para solado?
...wood flooring	...el parqué?
...blinds	...los estores?
...curtains	...las cortinas?
...curtain tracks	...los rieles de cortinas?
...net curtains	...los visillos?
we are looking for...	buscamos...
...an armchair	...una butaca
...some chairs	...unas sillas
...a table	...una mesa
...a bookcase	...una estantería de libros

...some cupboards	...unos armarios
...a sofa-bed	...un sofá-cama
...a bed	...una cama
...a bedside cabinet	...una mesilla de noche
...a chest of drawers	...una cómoda
...a wardrobe	...un armario (de ropa)
...duvets	...unos edredones
...a mattress	...un colchón
...some pillows	...unas almohadas

El jardín – the garden

Talking to los albañiles – the builders (Track 19)

can you build...	¿Vd. puede construir...
...a panelled fence	...una valla de paneles?
...a gate	...un portal?
...a wall	...un muro?
...a swimming pool...	...una piscina...
the pool needs...	la piscina necesita...
...coping (for edge of pool)	...un borde
...a cover	...una cobertura
...a pump	...una bomba
...a safety fence	...un cerco de protección
...a sand filter	...un filtro de arena
...some steps	...una escalera

Shopping for el jardín – the garden (Track 20)

where can I find...	¿dónde se puede(n) encontrar...
...deck chairs	...las tumbonas?
...folding chairs	...las sillas plegables?
...garden lights	...las balizas?
...a patio heater	...un calefactor de patio?

...a sand pit	...un cajón de arena?
...an extension lead	...una extensión eléctrica?
...a garden brush	...una escoba de jardín?
...a hedge trimmer	...un cortasetos?
...a hose	...una manguera?
...an incinerator	...un incinerador?
...mowers	...los cortacéspedes?
...potting trowels	...los desplantadores?
...rakes	...los rastrillos?
...a ride-on mower	...un tractorcito?
...a roller for a hosepipe	...un enrollador para mangueras?
...a sprinkler	...un aspersor?
...a water barrel	...un bidón?
...seeds	...las semillas?
...shears	...las tijeras de jardín?

Appendix

la inversión – investment

Buying for investment

If you are thinking of buying property in Spain as an investment, think long-term, think off-plan, or think again.

At the time of writing (2007), the Spanish house price boom, that had seen prices double between 2000 and 2005 has come to an end. The Spanish economy has slowed, reducing native pressure on prices, and the UK property boom – which exported house price inflation to the prettier parts of much of Europe – is well past its peak. Prices are still rising, but more slowly overall, and not at all in some areas. Along the southern coasts, where people have made substantial capital gains in the recent past, properties are now rarely fetching their asking prices and have been taking an average of three years to sell.

Having said that, in the long term, in Spain as in the UK, house prices have risen ahead of inflation, and property has shown a better return than most other forms of investment – and it is reasonable to expect that to continue. In the long term, property in Spain must be a good investment – it's a simple matter of climate and demographics. Brits – and the Dutch and Germans, but especially Brits – want a place in the sun, and Spain fits the bill nicely. It's got the sun; it's only a couple of hours away (by cheap flights); the language is not a problem because there are plenty of Brits already down there and lots of the locals speak English; it's in the EU so there are no restrictions on us buying houses, living there or using their health services, etc.; and you can get fish and chips and warm beer in the more popular spots. Current estimates are that around 750,000 Brits already own a property in Spain, either for holidays, retirement or a new life in the sun, and according to the opinion polls, 2 to 3 million more of us would like to buy a place there. As long as you buy the sort of property that other sun-seekers would like, in the sort of area that they would like to live in, then you should have got yourself a solid long-term investment.

Of course, you can lose money if you are not careful. There are two main dangers: paying too much in the first place, and having to sell in a hurry. Even if you get the price right when buying, you need a sale price of 25% or so higher to show any real profit, once the fees and taxes and other costs are taken into account. On current trends, this could take 5 years or more.

Buying off-plan is the only way to get a short-term return on property – and that is in no way guaranteed. The theory is this: you agree to buy the apartment (which is what it normally will be) from the developer when it only exists on the plan, and you pay a 10 or 15% deposit. You will be required to come up with further payments at different stages in the building process – perhaps totalling half the purchase price. You won't need to find the rest of the cash until completion – and you may be able to sell even before that. If you get it right, the development will be so popular that people will be queuing up to buy it off you, giving you a nice quick profit. If you get it wrong, you will be left with an expensive white elephant – and since the end of the last big property boom, it's been harder to pick winners.

At the moment, there are a lot of new developments stimulated partly by the recent price boom, and partly by the prospect of a new building code that will push up the cost of construction. In the more popular areas, especially the concrete shorelines of the southern Costas, there is currently an oversupply, with far more properties than buyers – so there's no chance of quick off-plan profits there. (And little prospect of any kind of capital gain, except in the very long term.)

If you want to buy as an investment, there are better places than Spain – and better Spanish-speaking places (see page 187). If you want a property that will also be a retirement or holiday home, as well as an investment, there are three approaches that you might like to investigate: 'the long view', 'restore a ruin' and 'go for golf'.

If you take the long view, you are looking ahead 10 or 20 years or more, hoping for capital growth overall, but with some rental income to help offset the costs while the property appreciates. For this you should buy a house or apartment, in good condition, in an attractive area where there are lots of activities for holidaymakers. A pool is pretty well essential, but the property does not have to be on the coast. Inland is good, especially if there are golf courses, horse-riding, good walking country or spectacular views close by. An unusual house or other distinguishing features will increase rentability.

There's potential in restoring ruins. The Spanish countryside has lots of empty *fincas* (farmhouses) looking for someone to give them a new lease of life. It is possible to pick up a run-down one for £30,000, spend £30,000 on modernising it and sell it for £100,000. Possible, but you need to know what you are doing. In some cases these properties really are ruins, where 'pull down and rebuild' is the only sensible option. Others just need bringing into the 21st century, but even that is not as simple as it might sound. The problem is that rural Spain as a whole is not yet into the 21st century – in parts it's barely out of the 19th. Pitfalls for the unwary are legion; here are just a few.

- Lots of properties are not properly documented. Historically they have been sold or transferred to relatives, friends or neighbours and the transaction has been noted verbally. The paper deeds for a property – if they exist at all – may bear little relation to the boundaries on the ground.
- *Fincas* can be small – think in terms of a shepherd's shack rather than a hidalgo's hacienda – and planning restrictions are stiff in the Spanish countryside. Don't expect to be able to extend a *finca* beyond its original footprint.

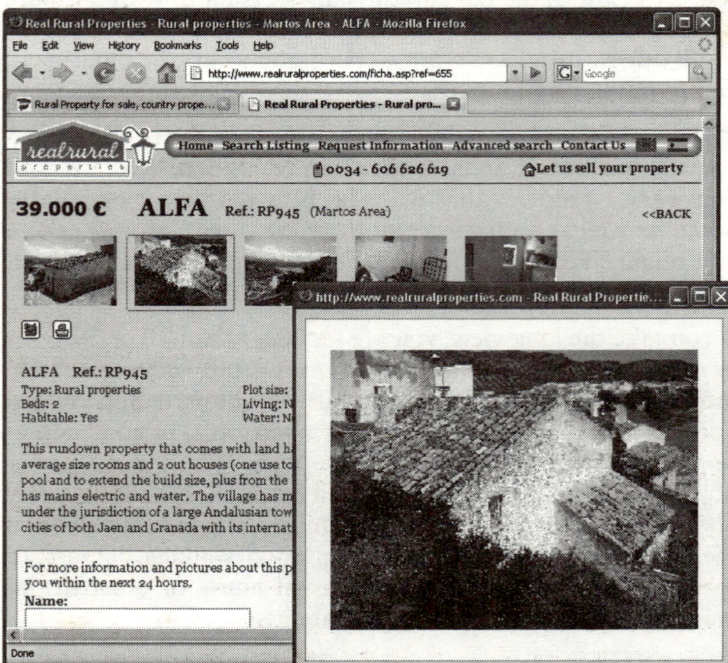

The thing about restoring ruins is that, if you don't mind roughing it at the start, and getting your hands dirty, you can get a lot more for your money.

- You must be ready to deal with the local planners and builders yourself, which means learning at least something of the language. There are expat British builders out there, but they have a bit of a reputation for being expensive and unreliable. There are also expat and English-speaking agents who can manage the works for you, but their fees will eat deep into any profit.

Try these sites for rural properties – in all sorts of conditions from ruins to newly built.

www.realruralproperties.com

www.countrypropertiesinspain.com

www.spanish-inland-properties.com

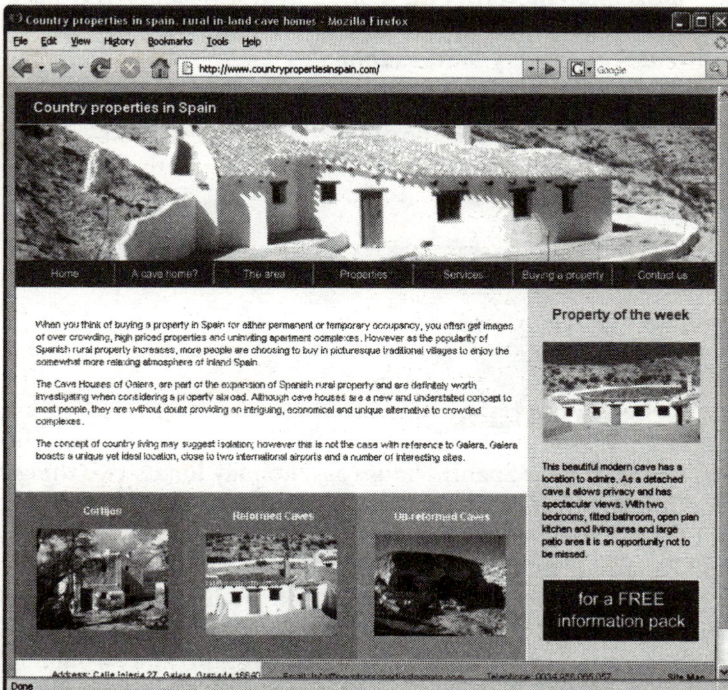

If you want an unusual house, how about a cave house? These are not as primitive as they might sound – in fact they can be very cosy, comfortable and quite stylish. Go to www.countrypropertiesinspain.com and find out more.

I've labelled the third approach 'go for golf', though it's actually broader than that. Apartments, chalets and villas in holiday park developments – which tend to centre on golf courses – may currently offer the best potential for a decent return on investment in Spain. Well-maintained, secure, holiday communities should have a lasting appeal, and produce better than average capital growth in the longer term. These developments almost always offer a rental management service, with some guaranteeing a minimum rental income. Though prices are lower inland than on the coast, golf complex apartments are not cheap – a 3-bed apartment will typically cost over £250,000. Neither short nor long-term profits are guaranteed, of course, so you have to pick carefully. For long-term rental income and capital growth, you need a good management company that will bring in the visitors and look after the property. For short-term profits you need projects where prices really will rise during their construction, and these can be very hard to spot.

These sites specialise in new developments. Browse them to get an idea of prices and specifications, but don't even think about buying until you have researched the project and the surrounding area very thoroughly.

www.europropertyguide.com

www.sunenterprise.co.uk

www.hiperprop.com

Holiday rentals

If you bought your Spanish house as a holiday home, two things should follow from this: (1) it's in a nice place to have a holiday, and (2) it will be empty for much of the year. Why not rent it out? Potential rental income varies hugely, of course, depending upon the size, position and features of the house, and on the time of year, and in the quality of the marketing that brings in the visitors. A large family-sized villa with a private swimming pool in the Costa Blanca could rent out at £1500 or more per week in the high season; 3-bedroom apartments in the Costa del Sol are currently asking £300 a week. But it will not be every week. There are now so many holiday homes/investment properties in Spain, that the rental market is very competitive – and in places there is a huge oversupply. Unless your property has

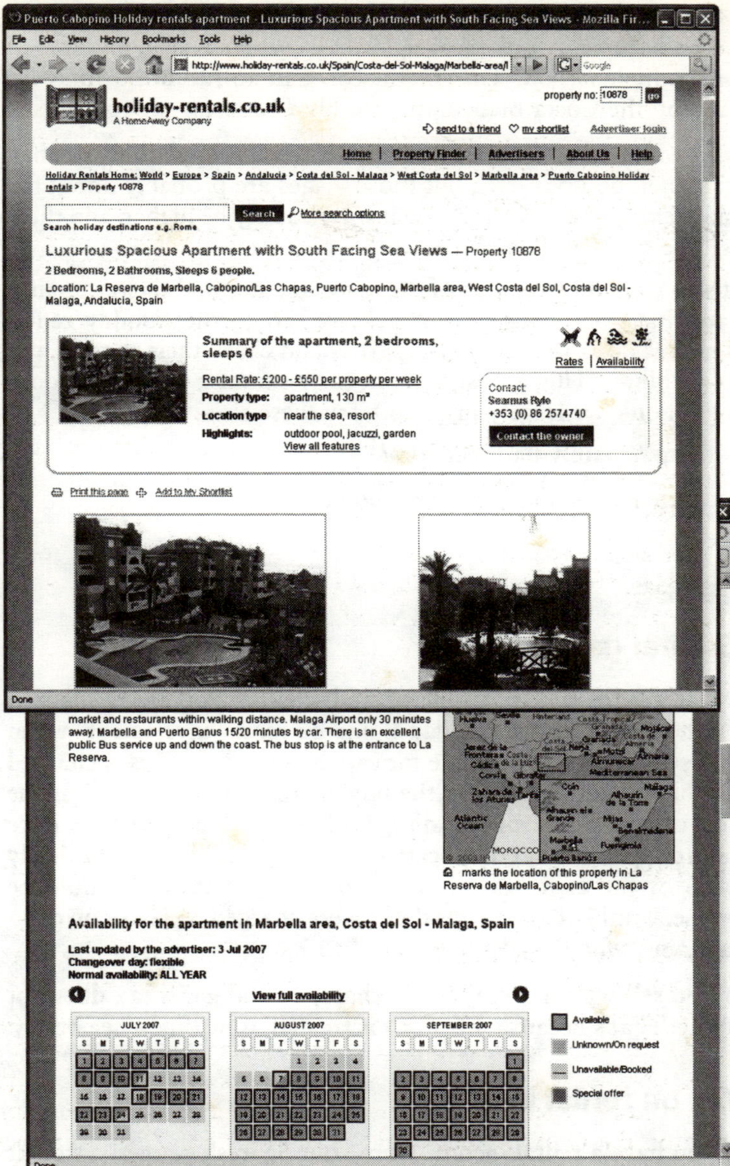

Research your market! Check the bookings of similar properties to get an idea of potential rental income. At the start of June, this 4 bedroom cottage had bookings for only five weeks in summer, and would have earned £2500 – before costs – in total that year. Similar properties at other sites showed the same level of activity.

something special, and you market it well, you should not count on an occupancy rate of over 10% – 5 weeks a year, and not all in the high season. That might bring in £5000 or so for your villa on the Costa Blanca, or possibly £1500 for an apartment.

You will need to find someone local to act as keyholder, cleaner, gardener, poolboy, etc., but those wages are probably about the main extra costs – your house insurance may be higher, and there will be more wear and tear on the contents.

If you want a better idea of the rental income and the occupancy rate that your house might achieve, go to the holiday rental websites, look for similar properties and check their charges and availability. (This is best done in early summer when the bookings should be largely in place.) Try these sites:

http://spain.villadirect.com/

http://www.holiday-rentals.co.uk

Taxes

Capital gains

Whatever the type of property, and whether you are resident in the house, or it is a holiday home or rental investment, when you sell it you will be liable for capital gains tax. This is charged on the difference between the buying and selling prices, less the cost of any significant building work – for which you must have full receipts. It is a complicated tax to calculate, but is basically 18% of the gain, less an allowance for inflation. It could be worse. Until 2007, non-residents were charged 35% tax on capital gains, while residents paid only 15%.

If you sell within a year of purchase, capital gains tax does not apply. That's because the profit is treated as income – see below.

Tax on rental income

If you have a rental income from your Spanish property, then it is subject to tax.

- If you are a Spanish resident, then 50% of the rent will be allowed as necessary expenses, and the remaining 50% added to your other income and subject to normal income tax.

- If you are a non-resident, the Spanish taxman will take a flat 25% of all rental income, with no allowable deductions. And what's left will be subject to UK income tax.

Income tax

Income earned in Spain is taxable in Spain, which is fair enough. If you become a Spanish resident, you will be able to claim a tax-free personal allowance. This will be a minimum of €5000 or substantially more if you have children living at home or you are over 65. Income above this is taxable on a sliding scale, starting at 24% for the first €16,000 and rising to 43% for anything over €56,000.

If you are a non-resident, any profit from the sale of a property within a year of purchase – which applies to off-plan sales – will be counted as income and subject to a flat 35% tax.

Beware the Hacienda

The tax authorities, known as the Hacienda, have been clamping down heavily on tax avoidance these last few years, and non-residents/foreign home owners – who have been among the worst offenders in the past – have been selected for special attention. If you don't pay, and get caught, then you will be faced with fines and interest charges on top of the unpaid tax. This applies to all taxes – on capital gains, wealth, rental and any other Spanish income.

Argentina

Sunny climate, good food and wine, lots of English speakers, even though Spanish is the local language (sounds like Spain) and with good investment potential (must be somewhere else). Latin America has been subject to increasing investment interest in the last few years, with the main focus on Argentina.

Argentina is the second largest country in South America, and rich in agricultural produce and raw materials. The population is largely of European origin, and the capital, Buenos Aires, has such a European feel that it is sometimes called 'the Paris of Latin America'. The city has a rich cultural life with around 300 theatres, an opera house, and over 100 galleries and museums.

Argentina has had periods of military rule, but has been a stable democracy since 1983. An economic crisis in 2001–2002 provoked a crash in property prices and a devaluation of the peso, but the country has bounced back, with GDP growing by around 9% a year. Property prices have recovered, but are still low and are very low for outside investors because the currency is undervalued. (There is an extra bonus for British investors at present – property is priced in dollars, and the dollar is currently at an all-time low against the pound.)

There are hundreds of small local estate agents in Argentina – but as an outsider, you would do better to stick to the bigger, well established firms. Some of them, like Reynolds, have English-language websites and cater for foreign investors.

Overseas investors are welcome, and not subject to any restrictions on the movement of money into and out of the country, though there are some practical obstacles to overcome. To buy in Argentina, you must register with the tax authorities; when you come to sell, you must have a certificate to show that your local property taxes are fully paid – the costs are minimal, but the bureaucracy is labyrinthine. All property purchases are in cash – literally bundles of US dollars handed across the table; the estate agent industry is unregulated; and corruption is all too common in government departments. But with a good local lawyer, and an established estate agent, these problems should be soon overcome.

If you want to buy purely as an investment, then an apartment in Buenos Aires is probably the best choice, because it will give you a good long-term rental return while it is appreciating in value. If you also want to use the property as a holiday home have a look at the 'gated communities' – country clubs – on the outskirts of the city. These are very popular and have good short-term rental and capital growth potential.

Taxes, fees and the buying process

The buying process is almost the same as in Spain – the main difference being that you must have your tax registration before you can buy, which will add a few weeks to the timescale. Allow 3 to 6 months from start to finsh.

Payments are normally made in cash, and in dollars. When you transfer money into Argentina it must be converted to pesos, and it must then be converted to dollars when taken out. In total the bank will charge you 5% or more of the value.

Lawyer's fees can be up to 3% and you will also have to pay the estate agent's commission – typically 3%, and a share of the transfer tax (1.5%). Overall, allow an additional 15% on the purchase price for the buying costs.

For the ongoing costs, the annual local property tax is 0.75% of the assessed value, plus accountant's fees, say £250.

On the plus side, there is no capital gains tax, and only a small transfer tax when you sell.

Some useful websites

Reynolds Propiedades, estate agents:

www.homes.com.ar

ApartmentsBA, estate agents, specialising in apartment rentals:

www.apartmentsba.com

Mendoza; English-language directory and guide for Argentina:

Web: www.wtmendoza.com

Lexicon: la inversión – investment

alquiler (m)	rent
apartamento (m)	apartment
contrato (m)	lease
desembolso (m) inicial	deposit
hipoteca (f)	mortgage
impuesto (m) sobre la plusvalía	capital gains tax
interés (m)	interest
inversión (m)	investment
IVA	VAT
patrimonio (m)	wealth tax
promotor (m) inmobiliario	developer
realización (f)	completion
renta (f)	income
segunda vivienda (f)	second home
seguro (m)	insurance

English–Spanish quick reference

apartment	apartamento (m)
capital gains tax	impuesto (m) sobre la plusvalía
completion	realización (f)

deposit	desembolso (m) inicial
developer	promotor (m) inmobiliario
income	renta (f)
insurance	seguro (m)
interest	interés (m)
investment	inversión (f)
lease	contrato (m)
mortgage	hipoteca (f)
rent	alquiler (m)
second home	segunda vivienda (f)
VAT	IVA – Impuesto sobre el Valor Añadido
wealth tax	patrimonio (m)

Brazilian Portuguese
Bridge
British Empire, The
British Monarchy from Henry VIII, The
Buddhism
Bulgarian
Business Chinese
Business French
Business Japanese
Business Plans
Business Spanish
Business Studies
C++
Calculus
Calligraphy
Cantonese
Car Buying and Maintenance
Caravanning
Card Games
Catalan
Change and Crisis Management
Chess
Chi Kung
Chinese Medicine
Christianity
Classical Music
Coaching
Cognitive Behavioural Therapy
Cold War, The
Collecting
Computing for the Over 50s
Consulting
Copywriting
Correct English
Counselling
Creative Writing
Cricket
Croatian
Crystal Healing
CVs
Czech
Danish
Decluttering
Desktop Publishing
Detox
Digital Home Movie Making
Digital Photography
Dog Training
Drawing
Dream Interpretation
Dutch
Dutch Conversation
Dutch Dictionary
Dutch Grammar
Eastern Philosophy
Electronics
English as a Foreign Language
English for International Business
English Grammar
English Grammar as a Foreign Language
English Vocabulary
Entrepreneurship
Estonian
Ethics
Excel 2007
Feng Shui
Film Making
Film Studies
Finance for Non-Financial Managers
Finnish
First World War, The
Fitness
Flash 8
Flash MX
Flexible Working
Flirting
Flower Arranging
Franchising
French
French Conversation
French Dictionary
French for Homebuyers
French Grammar
French Phrasebook
French Starter Kit
French Verbs
French Vocabulary
Freud
Gaelic
Games Programming
Gardening

Genetics
Geology
German
German Conversation
German Grammar
German Phrasebook
German Verbs
German Vocabulary
Getting Pregnant
Globalization
Go
Golf
Good Study Skills
Great Sex
Greek
Greek Conversation
Greek Phrasebook
Green Parenting
Growing Your Business
Guitar
Gulf Arabic
Hand Reflexology
Happiness
Hausa
Herbal Medicine
Hieroglyphics
Hindi
Hindi Conversation
Hinduism
History of Ireland, The
Home PC Maintenance and Networking
How to DJ
How to Run a Marathon
How to Win at Casino Games
How to Win at Horse Racing
How to Win at Online Gambling
How To Win At Poker
How to Write A Blockbuster
Human Anatomy & Physiology
Hungarian
Icelandic
Improve Your French
Improve Your German
Improve Your Italian
Improve Your Spanish
Improving your Employability
Indian Head Massage
Indonesian
Instant French
Instant German
Instant Greek
Instant Italian
Instant Japanese
Instant Portuguese
Instant Russian
Instant Spanish
Intellectual Property
Internet, The
Internet and Email for the Over 50s, The
iPods and iTunes
Irish
Irish Conversation
Irish Grammar
Islam
Israeli-Palestinian Conflict, The
Italian
Italian Conversation
Italian for Homebuyers
Italian Grammar
Italian Phrasebook
Italian Starter Kit
Italian Verbs
Italian Vocabulary
Japanese
Japanese Conversation
Java
JavaScript
Jazz
Jewellery Making
Judaism
Jung
Kama Sutra, The
Keeping Aquarium Fish
Keeping Pigs
Keeping Poultry
Knitting
Korean
Latin American Spanish
Latin
Latin Dictionary

Latin Grammar
Latvian
Leadership
Letter Writing Skills
Life at 50: For Men
Life at 50: For Women
Life Coaching
Linguistics
LINUX
Lithuanian
Magic
Mahjong
Malay
Managing IT for Small Business
Managing Stress
Managing Your Own Career
Mandarin Chinese
Mandarin Chinese Conversation
Marketing
Marx
Massage
Mathematics
Meditation
Middle East Since 1945, The
Modern China
Modern Hebrew
Modern Persian
Mosaics
Music Theory
Mussolini's Italy
Nazi Germany
Negotiating
Nepali
New Testament Greek
NLP
Norwegian
Norwegian Conversation
Old English
One-Day French
One-Day French – the DVD
One-Day German
One-Day Greek
One-Day Italian
One-Day Portuguese
One-Day Spanish
One-Day Spanish – the DVD
Origami
Owning a Cat
Owning A Horse
Panjabi
PC Networking for your Small Business
Personal Safety and Self Defence
Philosophy
Philosophy of Mind
Philosophy of Religion
Photography
Photoshop
PHP with MySQL
Physics
Piano
Pilates
Planets
Planning Your Wedding
Polish
Polish Conversation
Politics
Portuguese
Portuguese Conversation
Portuguese for Homebuyers
Portuguese Grammar
Portuguese Phrasebook
Positive Pregnancy
Postmodernism
Pottery
PowerPoint 2007
PR
Presenting
Project Management
Psychology
Quick Fix French Grammar
Quick Fix German Grammar
Quick Fix Italian Grammar
Quick Fix Spanish Grammar
Quick Fix: Access 2002
Quick Fix: Excel 2000
Quick Fix: Excel 2002
Quick Fix: HTML
Quick Fix: Windows XP
Quick Fix: Word
Quilting
Recruitment

Reflexology
Reiki
Relaxation
Retaining Staff
Romanian
Running Your Own Business
Russian
Russian Conversation
Russian Grammar
Sage Line 50
Sanskrit
Screenwriting
Second World War, The
Serbian
Setting Up A Small Business
Shorthand Pitman 2000
Sikhism
Singing
Slovene
Small Business Accounting
Small Business Health Check
Songwriting
Spanish
Spanish Conversation
Spanish Dictionary
Spanish for Homebuyers
Spanish Grammar
Spanish Phrasebook
Spanish Starter Kit
Spanish Verbs
Spanish Vocabulary
Speaking On Special Occasions
Speed Reading
Stalin's Russia
Stand Up Comedy
Statistics
Stop Smoking
Sudoku
Swahili
Swahili Dictionary
Swedish
Swedish Conversation
Tagalog
Tai Chi
Tantric Sex
Tap Dancing
Teaching English as a Foreign Language
Teams & Team Working
Thai
Theatre
Time Management
Tracing Your Family History
Training
Travel Writing
Trigonometry
Turkish
Turkish Conversation
Twentieth Century USA
Typing
Ukrainian
Understanding Tax for Small Businesses
Understanding Terrorism
Urdu
Vietnamese
Visual Basic
Volcanoes
Watercolour Painting
Wedding, Your
Weight Control through Diet & Exercise
Welsh
Welsh Dictionary
Welsh Grammar
Wills & Probate
Windows Vista
Wine Tasting
Winning at Job Interviews
Word 2007
World Faiths
Writing a Novel
Writing Crime Fiction
Writing for Children
Writing for Magazines
Writing a Play
Writing Poetry
Xhosa
Yiddish
Yoga
Zen
Zulu